A LITTLE
PIECE
OF LIGHT

A LITTLE PIECE OF LIGHT

A MEMOIR OF HOPE, PRISON, AND A LIFE UNBOUND

DONNA HYLTON

WITH KRISTINE GASBARRE

hachette BOOKS

NEW YORK BOSTON

Hachette Books
Hachette Book Group
1290 Avenue of the Americas
New York, NY 10104
hachettebooks.com
twitter.com/hachettebooks

First edition: June 2018

Hachette Books is a division of Hachette Book Group, Inc.

The Hachette Books name and logo are trademarks of Hachette Book Group, Inc.

The publisher is not responsible for websites (or their content) that are not owned by the publisher.

The Hachette Speakers Bureau provides a wide range of authors for speaking events. To find out more, go to www.hachettespeakersbureau.com or call (866) 376-6591.

Library of Congress Cataloging-in-Publication Data

Names: Hylton, Donna, author. | Gasbarre, Kristine, author.
Title: A little piece of light: a memoir of hope, prison, and a life unbound / Donna Hylton, with Kristine Gasbarre.
Description: First edition. | New York: Hachette Books, [2018]
Identifiers: LCCN 2017055248| ISBN 9780316559256 (hardcover) | ISBN 9781478922391 (audio download) | ISBN 9780316559218 (ebook)
Subjects: LCSH: Hylton, Donna. | Women prisoners—United States—Biography. | Female offenders—Rehabilitation—United States—Biography. | Prison reformers—United States—Biography. | Corrections—United States. | Criminal justice, Administration of—United States.
Classification: LCC HV9468.H95 A3 2018 | DDC 365/.9747277092 [B]—dc23
LC record available at https://lccn.loc.gov/2017055248

Printed in the United States of America

LSC-H

10 9 8 7 6 5 4 3 2 1

To Sr. Mary Nerney, CND, and all the women still at Bedford.

CONTENTS

FOREWORD

I have known Donna for over a decade. I knew her inside prison and I know her as a free woman. I know her more deeply than I have known many people, as I had the honor and privilege to travel with her in our writing group at Bedford Hills Correctional Facility for many years as she mined the depths of her own history, excavated the abuse done to her, and reckoned with her anger, shame, self-hatred, and guilt. I had a front-row seat witnessing Donna face her crime and probe her role and take responsibility and find the connections to her own trauma and history.

Now she has written a powerful and important book. It is a book that has arrived exactly at the moment it is needed. It is a book that has arrived as millions of women in America purge their stories and pain and memories and body traumas, and men reckon with their deeds and sexual misconduct. It has arrived at a moment of cultural excavation and hopefully a cultural transformation.

Donna's story shows with clarity and heart and painful personal detail the tragic trajectory of sexual violence. One has to ask about most women who have been sexually abused: At what point did they vacate their bodies and their lives? Was it the moment of the first violation? The second? In Donna's case, it is clear that she was long gone by the time the recurring acts of violence against her began.

Sexual violence forces us out of our bodies and ourselves. It lays us vulnerable to be controlled and further abused as our agency is stolen from the onset. It robs us of our "sense of goodness"; and once that is taken, so is our confidence and vision of a future. I know in my own case I became the darkness that was injected inside me. And then I lived in darkness for many years.

The time I spent at Bedford Hills, listening to stories, witnessing the layers of violence and violations women have suffered, made me aware that our prisons are filled with women who have been hurt and broken and abandoned. The statistics are shocking.

The overwhelming majority of women in prison are survivors of domestic violence. Three quarters of them have histories of severe physical abuse by an intimate partner during adulthood, and 82 percent suffered serious physical or sexual abuse as children. Nearly 8 in 10 female mentally ill inmates reported physical or sexual abuse. And 57.2 percent of females report abuse before their admission to state prison. Nearly 6 in 10 women in state prisons had experienced physical or sexual abuse in the past, and 69 percent reported that the assault occurred before age 18.

We have constructed a system that extols punishment over care and transformation, that categorically refuses to look at the economic, racial, psychological, or emotional roots of violence and forever perpetuates this violence through further institutional abuse.

The heartbreaking thing is that so many women woefully acknowledge that prison is the first place they ever felt safe, ever had time to think. So many women in my writing group at Bedford Hills came to realize in the course of our exploration how little choice they ever felt they had in their lives. Things just happened. The wheels of pain, exploitation, and violation moved them, and they never had a sense they could direct their own lives. And the wheels were set in dangerous motion from the first moment they were invaded, raped, beaten, tortured, or discarded. Because they were alone, without interventions or protections, they were propelled unwittingly toward a catastrophic cliff.

Donna was used and abused and abandoned from an early age. She had little control over her destiny or her even choosing her own family. She was spit out into the world as so many people continued to have their way with her. She lived in a state of perpetual terror, confusion, and powerlessness.

This book is a call for deep examination. It begs us to look at young women—particularly those on the margins who remain invisible, where terrible things happen over and over. Donna was a brilliant, beautiful young woman. Her beauty was used against her time and time again. She was never allowed or encouraged to fulfill her intellectual prowess as her self-esteem and sense of goodness had already been demolished.

Donna's story highlights the fact that when the abuse of women in prison is treated and addressed, when inmates are able to tell their stories and explore what led them to prison, when they are given time and support to take responsibility for their crimes, they not only change but can become the most productive members of society.

My hope for Donna and her book is that it will be our wake-up call. Through reading *A Little Piece of Light* we will understand that Donna's story is the story of thousands of women, if not millions, who were ravaged before they had a chance to be born, who were propelled toward violence or violent situations by the incessant violence done to them.

We have a choice as a country. We can keep the industrial punishment machine alive, continue to demean, dehumanize, and hurt the most wounded. We can guarantee that they never find a way out of the maze of darkness. Or as Donna's story so brilliantly illustrates, we can offer attention, time, and care before and after that catastrophic moment occurs in women's lives.

—Eve Ensler

PREFACE

"Say his name."

I stand in front of the stainless-steel mirror in my cell in the solitary housing unit. My face is bare of any makeup—there is nothing covering this up, no making it any prettier. This is me, facing myself. Facing what I did. "Say his name," I whisper at the mirror. *"SAY HIS NAME!"*

I brace myself to sit on the slab of metal that serves as my bed in my cell. "Thomas Vigliarolo," I whimper. *"His name is Thomas Vigliarolo!"* The crescendo of sobs breaks me. "I'm sorry, Mr. V!" I call out. Weak from the years of carrying this weight, my voice drops again to a whisper as I beg for his forgiveness. "I am so sorry, Mr. V. I am so, so sorry that I didn't help you."

Cries echo throughout the unit—my own, and the cries of the women around me. In this place, our cries are our only release. We cry for ourselves, and we cry for each other. With each other.

For many of us here, imprisonment began long before the day we registered in prison. Feeling trapped and isolated began years before we found ourselves confined to a six-by-eight cinder block room with no clock to mark the time. A prison worse than any government facility is the feeling that nobody loves you. Nobody wants you. You belong nowhere. As the men in my life told me from the time I was a child: *Donna, you are nobody, and nobody will ever love you.* Years...decades...lives of abuse and neglect spurred many of us to make one desperate decision that finally, ultimately led us here. Too often, by the time a woman commits a crime, her only goal has been survival.

For that lapse in judgment, that poor decision—that mistake—it's likely she will forever suffer the worst prison of all: the inability to forgive herself.

I'll never forget waking up to my friend's words: *He's not breathing.* It was a turn of events that I could not fathom. Even now, half a decade after leaving prison, not a day goes by that I don't think about Mr. Vigliarolo. Not a day goes by that I don't think of his family, the fear they must have felt as they imagined him in fear, wondering where he was for eleven nights and worried for what he might have been experiencing.

Say his name.

I'm sorry, Mr. V.

I know what it's like to fear for the safety of the person we love. Family is *protection*. I know this because on the day I gave birth, that was my fiercest vow to my daughter: *I'm not going to let anything bad happen to you.* And I know this because, beginning in my childhood, I lived a life of suffering and tough choices for two decades, until I finally found my family in the most unexpected place: prison. In spite of all the pain I've experienced in my life, I've never wanted anyone to die. But it is here, in this most unlikely place, that I found the protection and support I needed to turn my life around.

I am Donna—but here, for twenty-seven years, I was inmate #86G0206.

This is my story.

THE PRISONER OF BOYNTON AVENUE

I was three years old, barefoot against the chilled concrete floor in the back of a pub on William Street in my birthplace of Port Antonio, Jamaica, surrounded by blue lagoons, white sand beaches, waterfalls, and caves. Wafting in from a street vendor outside was the aroma of roasted meat wrapped inside steamed banana leaves. My tummy growled with hunger for something to eat. My heart yearned with hunger for attention…affection. As if suddenly aware of me while she and her sister discussed some business in the pub, which they ran together, my mummy picked me up and squeezed me closely to her. *"Oooh,"* she cooed, "I love you so much." I splayed my tiny fingers across her shoulders, feeling the way her coffee skin held the sun's heat even inside the cool of the dim bar.

At once, she released me toward the ceiling, my fall startling me when the breeze became my only security. The next second, I felt my mother's hands braced around my body. Again, she launched me into the air—and this time I giggled with the thrill of it. A third time, she swung me high, and I flew like a bird with my arms outstretched toward heaven, squealing in laughter. When I looked down for the safety of her hands, our eyes met, but in an instant it struck me that her hands were no longer in the air, anticipating my return.

I plummeted to the ground, my head *smack*ing the concrete floor.

Even now, fifty years later, the sheer shock of it stuns me. After a moment of numbness followed by confusion and fuzzy disorientation, the sensation set in, making it certain: my mummy let me fall.

I screamed in pain.

I screamed!

"What's wrong with you?!" my auntie scolded my mother. An argument erupted while I lay facedown, crying out, craving loving hands to pick me up and make this better.

This is my earliest memory. All these years later, my heart sinks to remember it. It remains a moment that symbolizes the first twenty years of my life: adult hands harming me instead of protecting me. A touch that I should have been able to trust, but could not.

William Street was two blocks from the water and therefore a lucrative hangout for locals looking to make a few dollars from the tourists who came to the beaches of Port Antonio. It was an area known for its laid-back Rastafarian spirit and its tropical fruits, flowers, butterflies, and birds. When I chased the mango hummingbirds into the fields on the edge of town, they showed me how to suck the nectar from the honeysuckle and morning glories. Fast and graceful, boundless and free, these creatures seemed magic to me.

My mother also believed in magic, but her fascination was different than mine. She was a devotee of the taboo practice of the West Indies called Obeah. Before it had been outlawed in the late 1700s, some observers of the religion believed it was a way to transmit harm to their slavemasters. They performed witchcraft and spells and sacrificed animals wildly and cruelly in public spaces. Some, like my mother, also used their children as real-life voodoo dolls.

I was born very shortly after Jamaica gained its independence from Great Britain in 1962. With the transition from British rule to independence came upheaval, a lack of systems, and centuries' worth of hurt and resentment. At that time, some laws in Jamaica weren't being enforced effectively. Systems also weren't very precise when it came to recording births or administering birth certificates—especially not for a mother like mine, who once told me that I was born on October 29, 1964 inside a cave. I'm more inclined to believe the part about the cave than I am to believe the specific date of birth. Only when I grew older and more detached from any sense of security at all did I realize I wish I'd had enough time with her to ask who my father was, why my skin was so much lighter than the skin of most of the people around me...or more about where I belonged, in general.

Back then, in Jamaica or anywhere, there also weren't insights or clear diagnoses for the problems my mother suffered. Today, we'd understand that her unpredictable mood swings, tenderness that turned to violence or indifference in a split second, were due to mental illness or a personality disorder, possibly bipolarism. One minute, she was bright-eyed and charismatic, while the next she was a monster, dunking me in scalding water, lashing me with a tree branch or rubber telephone wire that she found on the side of the road after a tropical storm snapped it to the ground. It was routine for her to burn me with fire and cut me with a knife. "Shut up!" she'd yell through gritted teeth while she lashed me. "You're unclean!" Sometimes, after she finished hurting me, she would soothe herself with deep breaths, then pull me close to hug me. "I am sorry," she'd say softly in remorse. "My baby...I am sorry." I would melt into her embrace, so achingly hungry to be loved in any moment.

Whether she was holding me close or harming me, there was no explanation for her emotional expression, no reason for her reactions. I simply nestled closely into her kindness when it was available and obeyed her when it wasn't. She was my mother—as a child, I needed her. She was beautiful and passionate, and over and over, I found it easy to forgive her. On some level even then, I understood that she loved me the best that she could.

But a child who never knows what will happen next will find some way—any way—to flee the moments of trauma and pain. I remember sitting in the corner of the cave where my mother and the Obeah priest would hold their rituals by firelight. "Come," my mother would motion to me. As a toddler, I would rise from my place against the wall of the cave and climb onto their stone table as their feathered costumes and head scarves now billowed above me. I kept my eyes on the glow of the fire on the rough rock ceiling overhead, focusing on that flicker with more and more concentration until their swaying and spells and cries out to their god sounded distant from me, as though I were sinking asleep and my ears became cushioned with protection from the sounds.

As my mother and her leader fell deep inside their prayers, their eyes closed and their voices hushed, I, too, would begin to disappear. In my mind, I began to rise up, out of my body, and look down on myself so that I was no longer feeling my experience from the inside, but observing it from the outside. I wanted to be out in the sunlight, chasing the butterflies. By the time I was four years old, blacking out to escape my reality had become my only way of emotionally surviving my dangerous childhood.

Early on, I devised a way to escape my mother's harm. As soon as I could walk, I learned to run—*fast*. I'd run from home into the streets, always the same bare feet, looking for a safe place as my hair fell heavy like ropes down my little back. Because my mother often wasn't home, I'd wander Port Antonio by myself, searching for some companion. Townspeople would allow me to duck inside their offices to hide from my raging mother while she made scenes in the street. To protect myself from loneliness, I created an imaginary friend—Michael—who would loyally roam with me to the shore.

At the age of six, I was offered a real escape. My mother introduced me to Roy and Daphne Hylton, a childless couple from

New York. Mummy explained that both the husband and wife came from families of great status in Jamaica. They had no children of their own, but Roy was known to bring little girls to the United States with the promise of possibility, of dreams, and a good education. When I met them, Roy and Daphne exchanged a glance and told me about a happy, magical place with parks, rides, laughs, and cotton candy. "We've just come from Disneyland," Daphne said. Her hair flipped up at the perimeter with precision; her skin was cocoa-colored, and she wore blue silk pants that landed smartly just about the ankle and a matching blouse, buttoned straight to the top, with carefully capped sleeves. Everything about her—right down to her nose—was slim and direct. "Would you like to travel there with us someday?"

I lowered my chin, timid about the idea of going anywhere with two grown-ups I didn't know. I turned to my mother, searching her face for her role in this, only to find an amusement in her eyes that seemed to urge me forward. Would she be coming, too?

For another moment, I stayed silent. "Do you know what Disneyland is?" Daphne's eyes were a see-through shade of brown when she bent to see me eye-to-eye—a nature of exchange that would later be rare between us. "It's a magical place for children."

"Magic?"

She stood tall again, indicating with her raised eyebrows that this was something I'd be silly to miss.

Standing in the clarity of the Jamaican sun, we all bought into Daphne's story about magic. I would trust Roy and Daphne just enough to step onto an airplane and fly to the place of promises and dreams…but before very long, my childhood would turn into a nightmare that would be impossible to escape, no matter how hard I would run.

The next time I meet Roy Hylton will be the last time I'll ever see my natural mother. In June 1972, four months before my eighth birthday, Roy passes my mummy a handful of money. I watch while in exchange, she hands him some papers. They'd already sent me for a haircut, where I counted each of my wild Caribbean braids as they fell to the ground, a piece of myself landing there with each one. I glance at the document in Roy's hand—the word PASSPORT written above a photograph of a little girl with wild, frizzy hair and eyes that look tired, sad…powerless. Doing my best to practice my reading from primary school, I read the words typed under her face: DONNA PATRICIA WALDEN.

Until this moment, I've never known my last name.

It's still daytime when Roy and I land at LaGuardia Airport, where adults bump into me with their suitcases as I follow Roy off the plane. The air in the taxi line smells like cigarettes and petrol, and when we get in a car that moves along into the street, the buildings here are so tall that I have to shield my eyes from the sun to take them in. Buses beep, the subway trains rattle the tracks above the ground, and steam rises from grates in the street. "What's that place?" I point.

From the front seat of the taxi, Roy looks up from the newspaper he's reading. "That's a playground," he says. Children run and swing and spin each other on the rides, shouting and squealing with laughter.

Is this Disneyland?

The taxi lets us out in front of a high, redbrick building with lots of windows and terraces all the way up to the top. "Where are we?" I quietly ask Roy.

"We're home."

Home? I think. *What is home?* "When are we going to Disneyland?"

And then there's my most pressing question: *When will I see my mummy in Jamaica again?*

Roy says nothing about Disneyland, or my mummy, or anything at all as we enter the double glass doors into the apartment building. Inside, two silver doors slide open when he pushes a glowing button on the wall. "Go on," he says. "Get on the elevator." Cautiously I step inside, and the doors slide closed behind us. When I catch my reflection, my eyes are worried. My hair is messy, like in the photograph on my passport.

Roy lets us into the apartment, and I look across the floor of the living room, hard tiles stretching across the floor, with the walls painted a beige shade of green. There stand a bench, a chair and sofa, a piano…and lots and lots of bookshelves. There's also a sliding glass door with a terrace that overlooks the world below.

Daphne, Roy's wife with the flipped-up hair, walks politely down the hall toward me. "I suppose you'll need to get acquainted around here the next few weeks," she tells me.

When are we going to Disneyland?

She walks me down the hall, past the bathroom and a wall of closets. Across from a bedroom with a big double bed is another bedroom, with a single bed. "This will be your room," she says. "Unless we have guests. Then you'll stay in the living room."

To do errands in the city we ride the subway, which moves and rocks and makes me feel so unsteady. All the people and distractions in the city have the same effect on me, and for weeks I walk around wide-eyed. I have so many questions: Why does everybody move so fast? Why are all the buildings so high? When will I see my mummy again?

And what about Disneyland?

Roy and Daphne take me to flea markets, where Roy shops patiently for furniture, guitar strings, and old shoes. "Why do you buy all these things?" I ask him.

"I fix and resell them," he says. "It's important to know how to bargain." I watch the thought and consideration in his face as he barters with the people who work at the flea market, just like they do in Jamaica. When they don't agree to the price he wants, he shrugs to me gently—always my cue that it's time we walk away. The salespeople usually catch on and take this opportunity as their last chance to negotiate a fair price. Roy's nature is not disrespectful or unkind... but he does have a masterful way of getting what he wants.

His warmth is subtle, but Daphne's feels nonexistent. On the walk home from the train as we pass by the playground, she warns me how I'm to behave when I begin to meet other children: I'm not allowed to have anyone over, nor am I allowed to call anyone— they ensure this with a lock on the phone. "You don't go outside,"

Daphne says one morning as she slips her arms into the sleeves of a suit jacket. "New York is not like Jamaica, do you understand? You don't just speak to everyone you meet on the street."

I nod. "Where are you going?" My voice comes out like a whisper.

"To work."

"Where do you work?"

"I'm a psychiatric social worker." She starts out the door and opens it back up to meet my eyes. "Be very quiet," she tells me. "Your father tends to get upset if there's noise in the house."

My father?

The heavy white steel door clicks closed behind her. I stare at it, wondering for how long she'll be gone. I take in my surroundings as classical music crackles through the speakers of the brown wooden radio. I stand in the center of their living room, looking around for something I can do. I take soft steps across the grayish-beige tiled floor toward the bookshelves, to not disturb Roy from the work he's doing in his bedroom down the hall, across from my bedroom. *He tends to get upset if there's noise in the house.* I don't want Roy to get angry with me. In fact, as I linger silently in the living room, I hope he'll forget that I'm even here.

As the sound of his hammer taps from down the hall, I quietly browse the bookcases for something that I can page through, something with pictures or small words. But shelf after shelf, there are no stories here for me. There are big, thick books too heavy to hold, with titles I can't pronounce. They're written by people with difficult names that I try my best to sound out from the reading

10

lessons I had in my first year of school in Jamaica: *Sigmund Freud, Friedrich Nietzsche.* There's also a book with the title *Crime and Punishment,* whose cover I study—a painting of a man in a shadowy room who seems to be ducking in the dark away from something that scares him.

I discover a whole row of paperback books that are small enough for me to hold in my lap. I pull one of them out from the shelf and gaze at a painted image of a shirtless man holding a woman who seems too distracted by kissing him to notice that her lavender dress is falling off. I close the book and listen again: the sounds of hammering and violins.

One Saturday, just after I've arrived, Daphne takes me to Lord & Taylor to get me clothes for the school year. We take the elevator down to the basement clearance racks, where I gaze toward racks of dresses with ribbons that tie at the waist. "No, Donna Patricia," Daphne says. "You have to dress nicely." Over her arm, she drapes pairs of long slacks that bell out at the ankle, like some of the ones she wears, and turtlenecks that coordinate with little button-up blazers and plaid blouses. We go to the shoes section, and I look at the Mary Jane shoes with a tiny heel and a strap that fastens across the top of the foot. Daphne buys me a pair of blue suede-and-patent-leather loafers.

Before the first day of school, she stands behind me in the bathroom and uses a fine-tooth comb to part my hair severely to one side. "You must excel at school," she tells me. I try to steady my neck to each tight pull as she forms multiple braids on my head and fastens each of them with a plastic barrette. "And we've allowed you to get familiar around here, but from now on, you'll have to earn points at home. Do you know what this means?"

I meet her eyes in the mirror's reflection.

"It means that you need to help out around the house. You'll have chores, and you'll have to wash up before bed and brush your teeth. You'll do just as your father and I say."

My father? I don't have a father.

"Remember that your father can have a short temper, and I'm very busy with my work." She drops her hands to her sides and stares at me in the mirror. "We expect the best from you, Donna Patricia. Do you understand?"

I nod, but the butterflies inside me swarm my belly in worry.

Minutes later, Daphne walks me through the apartment building's driveway and across the street to P.S. 93. "Look at her shoes!" one girl in my first grade class shouts as she points, and her friends all crowd around her, giggling. I look at their shoes, pretty brown sandals and shiny Mary Janes. *I knew these shoes were for boys.* "You don't look like anybody," one girl says. "Are you black, or are you white?"

"She's an alien!" another girl says.

I don't know what I am, so all I can think to tell them is this: "I'm from Jamaica."

"From Jamaica!" one yells, and turns to her friends. "She even talks funny!"

These become the last words that I'll utter out loud for weeks. My teacher, Miss Zano, gently calls on me in class and encourages me to speak up when I answer in a whisper. When the other kids laugh at my accent, Miss Zano corrects them. "Children, that's enough," she says. "Donna is very bright."

At recess, the girls in my class gather at the edge of the playground, where they've designated an area for taking turns to spin two jump ropes to play double Dutch. I watch them for just a moment before I find an empty corner of the playground to be by myself. With my eyes down and my knees held tight against my chest, I imagine running after the butterflies and the hummingbirds in the fields back home.

For the first few weeks of school, I keep to myself this way, until I learn that not even staying alone is a guarantee against conflict. One day as I'm sitting against the chain-link fence in the schoolyard, a group of three girls approaches me. One of them kicks her foot at me.

"Leave me alone!" I tell her.

"Don't step on my blue suede shoes!" she says. I look down at my shoes, embarrassed that they look like a boy's. Why does she have to make fun of me with a song that I like? "Aren't you going to say anything?" she says.

"She can't talk, she's not American!" says one of the girls behind her. "What is she, anyway?"

"Maybe this will make her talk." The first girl raises her hand and wails it, smacking me in the face. *That's it.* Feeling alone, like an outsider, and missing Jamaica and my mummy is all too much. When I stand up, I punch the first girl so hard that she falls down. I back off immediately, and the girls all run in the opposite direction, scared. They don't bother me again after that.

As I get more familiar being inside Roy and Daphne's home, there's not much sense of belonging there, either. After school, I have to sit in the stairwell of our apartment building to wait for Roy to get home from his errands. One afternoon while I'm locked out, I need to use the bathroom so desperately that I have no choice but to race to another floor to find a dark corner in the stairwell and use it to relieve myself. "May I please get a key?" I ask Daphne.

"Why do you need a key?"

"Because I don't have anywhere to go after school."

"Absolutely not," she says. "Only adults can have keys, and you are not an adult."

On weekend afternoons, the screams and laughter of neighborhood kids in the playground below are my only entertainment. For hours I stand with my arms over the balcony railing and rest my chin on them, watching while my chest aches to be with the other children. I am alone, the alien girl. I'm the child from nowhere—I have no one here.

Back in the living room, I sit listening to classical music and the opera, the sounds and voices on the radio keeping me company. As Roy's hammer pounds from back in the hallway, I see which words I can spell out of Daphne's Harlequin romance novels with the cartoony covers, like *Music on the Wind* and *A Wife for Andrew*.

I pull the Bible from the shelf, thick and dense, and read beautiful phrases from Proverbs and Psalms that talk about the promise of God's power. "Out of my distress I called on the Lord; the Lord answered me and set me free." I also like the story of Job, who experiences a lot of tragedy in his life but never fails to believe in God.

The lesson in Job's story is that sometimes we endure suffering for reasons that only God can understand, that God will always protect us as long as we remain faithful to Him.

From Daphne's dresser, I pick up a paperback book that interests me. On it is the photograph of a freckle-faced little boy, and the book is titled *Dibs in Search of Self.* "May I read this?" I ask Daphne.

With her back leaning against her headboard, she rests the book she's reading and pulls her glasses to the tip of her nose to look at me over the top of them. "You want to read that?"

I nod.

"That's fine," she says. "The woman who wrote it is a psychologist, like me."

Quickly, I grow immersed in the story about a little boy who's my age and doesn't play appropriately with other children. In school, he crawls around the classroom and acts out with tantrums. Other times, he isolates himself and doesn't want to speak at all. His parents bring him to a counselor who invites Dibs to play with games and toys. By playing together, the counselor discovers that Dibs is actually a very smart little boy, that he feels alone in life. *Maybe Dibs is magic.* Nobody can understand Dibs, but I can. I don't fit in anywhere, either.

In October 1972, just over a month after I begin first grade, I turn eight years old. Roy smiles subtly when he gives me coloring books and comic books to read. Meanwhile, Daphne reminds me, "You need to read the more advanced books, too." She marches out to get the dictionary and teaches me how to look up words from the comic books that I don't know. "The words are listed alphabetically, Donna Patricia," she says. "This should make it relatively simple for you to find." I glance at Roy, who wears no expression as his eyes meet mine. It seems we're developing a shared awareness for Daphne's rigidness. Book after book, she builds a small stack of the stories that she assigns me to read, usually on the topics of psychology and philosophy, death, and the meaning of existence. After I read *Crime and Punishment* by Dostoyevsky, she asks me to sit down and give her a verbal summary of the story. "Well," I tell her with an uncomfortable sigh. "The story made me feel very sad."

"So?" she says. "What was it about?"

"It's about a man who is treated very unkindly. It reminded me of something I read about concentration camps in your *Reader's Digest*," I tell her.

"Ah, yes," she says. "That was quite a compelling article." Her response to my emotional reaction is always academic, never maternal. "Remember," she reminds me, "if there's something you don't understand, you can always find the explanation in the dictionary or encyclopedia."

"What if I can't find it there—then can I ask you?"

"An intelligent girl doesn't ask others questions, Donna Patricia. We must learn to find our own solutions."

She begins to give me lessons in the languages she speaks: Italian; Portuguese, as her father is from Portugal; and the two particular languages that she would like me to speak whenever I'm at home, French and Spanish. A couple of months into first grade, Miss Zano informs Daphne that they're advancing me to second. Daphne is delighted and so our lessons at home grow even more hands-on. She shows me how to cut out patterns and stitch them onto fabric using her Singer sewing machine. She teaches me how to prepare recipes like Jamaican patties, rice and beans, and also okra, of which I'm not very fond. She also teaches me how to brew hot tea with a cup and saucer, and I begin to serve this to her and Roy in their bedroom each night while she reads and he watches the television. "Donna Patricia?" she calls from their bedroom. "Would you prepare the tea, please?" I bring the kettle to a boil and drape the tea bag string over each cup, dropping in a teaspoon of sugar after the water has begun to steam with the scent of dried tea leaves. I balance the saucers carefully as I make my way down the hallway, serving Daphne first, as she's taught me, and then Roy. "You know, in Japan," Daphne says, "tea time is quite a formal ceremony."

"Oh really?" I stand in the doorway, waiting to know if she intends to teach me more, but by now she's setting her teaspoon onto the saucer and taking her first sip. "Is it OK?" I ask her.

"It's fine," she says.

As my first Christmas with them approaches in 1972, I see Daphne warm up in a way I haven't seen before. Right after Thanksgiving, she says, "We'll have to get a beautiful tree for Christmas."

What's Christmas?

She leads Roy to a street corner vendor, where he buys a fresh pine tree tied with twine to make it easier to carry home by hand.

I watch and learn as Daphne makes an elaborate affair of decorating the tree with a string of teardrop-shaped, rainbow-colored bulbs and a sparkly tree topper star that plays Christmas songs. She leads me in arts and crafts projects, making ornaments out of pipe cleaners and paper. Orange-handled scissors move along to cut apart the cups of cardboard egg cartons, and we paste them back together in tiered rows to form a triangle Christmas tree. Then, Daphne and I paint all the cups green and decorate them with glitter. "This is fun, Mother," I tell her. I pause and glance out of the corner of my eye to see how she'll receive this title.

She softens, relaxes, smiles coyly at my choice of words. "It's fun for me, too, Donna Patricia."

When the first snow falls at Christmastime, I turn my palm up for the weightless crystalline flakes to fall into it. They melt into water as soon as they touch the pink of my palm. "What's it doing?" I ask Mother.

"This is snow," she says. "I suppose you've never seen it before, have you? You see, Donna Patricia, snow is water that's frozen. It precipitates from the sky..." She continues with her scientific explanation, but now the snowflakes are cooling my tongue and catching in the curl of my eyelashes.

Roy does not share in Mother's fondness for this time of the year. One evening, she plugs in the Christmas lights as the tree topper begins to sing its mechanical carols. Roy storms into the room and shoves me to the side before he throws Mother against the wall. He grabs the orange-handled scissors from our temporary craft table and holds them to her neck. *"Shut that fucking shit off right now,"* he hisses through clenched teeth. *"Do you understand me?"*

When he backs off, she releases herself slowly from the wall. He glares at Mother as she smooths herself over, then calmly crouches down to unplug the Christmas lights. "Fucking Catholics," he says, retreating down the hallway, where he was watching television in their bedroom. Suddenly, he stops and turns. "And your fucking books, too!" he yells to her. "You love those books more than you love me!" He slams the bedroom door behind him.

"Just be quiet," she whispers, shutting off the lights in the living room. Across the expanse of the dark room, she suggests, "Let's not upset him any more."

What any little girl needs to know most at this and every stage in her life is that she's so important that a parent would go to any lengths to protect her. Instead, as Roy's problems begin to surface, Daphne will deny that it's happening. To her, emotion is something we can dwell on or not, something we can shut off with as effortless a gesture as unplugging the Christmas lights. Inside the home of a woman who spent her entire career analyzing and diagnosing strangers, there was a disorder happening that would indicate a reality she could never—or, perhaps, simply *would* never—acknowledge.

This deficit in parenting, in guidance and protection, would go on to have more of an impact on my life than anything my adoptive mother taught me about foreign language, literature, the proper way for a woman to style herself, how to make clothes, or anything scholastic. In the months and years to come, the damage of what happens here will spur me into a spiral of choices that will become the devastating start to the story of my life.

The summer of 1974 marks two years since Roy brought me to New York. Daphne has taken me on a trip to Montreal to experience French culture, but, these days, there is no more talk of Disneyland. Daphne continues to dress me in outfits that match from my shoulders to my toes, like a green coat with a matching blouse underneath, and green corduroy pants. Adults always comment that I look "nice," but all I want is to look like other girls my age with their ribbons and shiny shoes. When we take the subway down to Macy's and Bergdorf Goodman, Mother always seems to catch me eyeing the Mary Janes. "Those shoes are unacceptable, Donna Patricia," she says. "Not even a tiny heel." She insists that my hair is braided to look "like a little girl," but from my blouses to the hem of my polyester slacks to the lessons on art, philosophy, and music that she presents to me in our home, it seems that her biggest goal is to make me into a miniature version of herself.

I go along with this because I will do anything to have her attention. Daphne doesn't hug me or tell me that she loves me, but emotionally, I need any interest she's willing to show me. I've taken to permanently calling her "Mother" because I need that nurturing figure in my life. When we sit together at the sewing machine or she asks me to summarize a book I've just read—"Speak in French, please"—I absorb her attention as care for me. And when I begin to experience the growing pains that come along with early puberty as

I approach age ten, I need her, or someone, to explain what's happening to me. "Mother?" I ask her shyly. "My body hurts."

"Where on your body?"

I point delicately toward my chest.

"Oh, alright," she laughs. "You're getting breasts, Donna Patricia, that's what girls experience. As a young lady, there are certain things you'll need to do now. You'll be sure to go to bed with panties on. If you keep your bra on all night, it will help to keep your breasts firm."

Both of these tips puzzle me. My adoptive mother is rarely personal with me, and I can't understand why these details about how I should take care of myself would matter. They make me feel embarrassed, more isolated in my uncertainty. As my body and my awareness about the truths of being female begin to change, there's still a great deal about my life here that I don't understand.

During my summer break from school at age nine when I'll be skipping from third to fifth grade, Roy brings me along on his outings. I follow him around his flea markets and thrift shops, peering at dolls and beautiful old clothes and furniture.

I like to explore the city in this way, but it's here that I begin to pick up on the quiet conversations Roy has with people in our neighborhood and in different parts of the city. I stand on our balcony, watching the children on the playground and overhearing the men who come into our apartment in the afternoons to meet with Roy. In the living room, they speak confidentially to him when they want a young, beautiful wife who will cook, clean, and do whatever they want. The men pay him even more to arrange all the necessary "paperwork" to have women brought in from Jamaica, since, as I understand, the United States is much stricter about letting people in than Jamaica is about letting people out.

I have yet to understand that my living here is the result of just this kind of arrangement, which I've heard them refer to as an "adoption." My natural mother used to tell me that the Hyltons had a lot of influence and connections in Jamaica and different parts of the world, and now I've learned that they have a lot of relatives in different places, too. When Roy's cousin comes from England to visit in the summer of 1974, two years since I arrived here, I finally start to understand how and why they really brought me here.

The summer that I'm nine and about to skip fourth grade to go directly into fifth, Roy and Daphne instruct me to move out of my bedroom so that Roy's cousin can use it for a couple of weeks. I spend these nights on the living room sofa bed, always making sure my bedroom is clear of their guest when I need to go in for clothes or other belongings. Then I slip into the bathroom to change. "Be careful not to take too much time in the bathroom while our guest is here, Donna Patricia," Mother says.

I'm always careful not to take too much time in the bathroom; after all, I still feel like a permanent guest here myself. One morning during this visit, I wake up on the sofa and feel terrible pain across my chest, the same kind of aching that I told Mother about. I check my bedroom to see if it's available for me to get some clothes out of the drawer, but Roy's cousin is inside with the door closed. In a state of agony that makes me want to double over, I turn and walk into the bathroom, hoping that maybe the heat and steam of a shower will relax the pain. But by the time I finish and dry off, the aching in my chest has grown even worse.

I wrap my towel around my body tightly and tiptoe back into the hallway. I *knock-knock* on Roy's bedroom door. He opens it partway and stares down at me. "Where are your clothes?" he says.

"I can't get in my room!" I tell him. "The door is closed. I'm sorry, I just..." I feel tears break over the brim of my eyelashes. "I hurt."

"You hurt?" he says. "You mean you're in pain?"

I nod.

"Come in," he says. He opens the door wider so I can walk in. Then he gestures for me to sit down on the bed. "Where does it hurt?" he asks.

Sheepishly, I hesitate. I feel him waiting for my answer, so I point to my chest area.

"It hurts there?"

I nod.

He pauses for a moment. "Do you want me to make you feel better?"

I look up at him, hoping he knows of some medicine I can take, or maybe just that he'll arrange with his cousin to let me rest in my bedroom. He asks me again: "Do you want me to make you feel better?"

I nod.

He opens the door to the walk-in closet that he and Mother

share. "Come in here," he says. When I look into the closet, it's dark. I don't understand what he's doing, but I follow him inside.

He pulls the closet door behind him. After my eyes adjust to the dark, I notice a little piece of light—a combination from the bedroom light and the sunshine coming through their window—that's breaking through the crack underneath the door.

Roy pulls my towel aside. "You're beautiful," he whispers in my ear. Then, he begins to touch me with his hands. My breasts sting at the pressure of his touch, and my stomach has suddenly gone sick. He rubs harder, not caring at all that I just told him I'm in pain.

He's hurting me.

After a moment of this, he begins to touch my breasts with his mouth.

He's hurting me.

It's too much for my mind to understand what's happening.

He's hurting me.

I don't want to upset Roy; I know there could be a knife or a pair of scissors hidden anywhere within his reach. I remain still, the air around us growing heavy in my belly with the smell of moth balls, old shoes, and the floral-spice smell of Daphne's signature fragrance, L'Air du Temps.

The air of time.

Almost as if in response to my thoughts, he whispers: "Don't tell your mother. You'll make her upset."

The entire time we're in the closet, I keep my eyes fixed on that little piece of light from the bedroom window that's slicing through the crack at the bottom of the closet door.

*　　*　　*

By the time Roy's cousin leaves to return to England, he's begun to take me into the closet every day. When I move back into my bedroom from the living room, he tells me not to close my bedroom door whenever I change. When it's just the two of us in the apartment, he stands in the doorway, licking his mustache and making suggestive grunting and kissing sounds while I discreetly try to dress with my back toward the door. At home, there's never a moment when I don't feel vulnerable and exposed.

If I felt isolated before all this began, the way Roy hurts me every day solidifies the fact that I can never have friends or confidantes here, or anywhere. "This is our secret," he reminds me on occasion. "Your mother will be very angry with you if she finds out."

However, as this secret between us carries on, Mother seems to be less present than ever, and more absorbed by her own pursuits whenever she is home. His secrets seem to drift him into his own separate world, while her studies pull her further outside. I remain some piece of currency—some pawn somehow between them. As I recall my very first interaction with them in Jamaica, I remember that Daphne expressed some aggravation about the length of the adoption process. It grows clearer to me that she wasn't fully on board with this arrangement; she didn't want to be bothered to mother someone else's daughter. Roy was the one who wanted to bring me here, and now, this innocent child's mind is beginning to understand the complicated reasons why.

I'm careful to do nothing to provoke his attention, but knowing that I run the risk of upsetting them both if I speak, I keep everything inside of me. I stay by myself. At nine, ten, and eleven years old, I take to the activities in school that don't call me to interact very much with my classmates. I pay attention in class and stay focused on my work, spending recess by myself, studying or reading. In phys ed class, I run fast, I run hard, as if my legs could save my life. On the school's running track, some of the other girls hover in groups and giggle about the boys. But I run. I zone out and lose myself, imagining my legs fast as the Jamaican humming-birds' wings, until it's time to change back into my dress clothes. In the locker room, I shower inconspicuously—quickly—with the front of myself turned toward a corner, ashamed of my body and fearful of any visible way the girls in my class might discern that I'm different because of what my adoptive father does to me each day.

In music class when our teacher instructs each of us to try out an instrument, I take up the clarinet and learn the notes with con-centration. In time, I practice some of the songs that I hear on the radio by the New York Philharmonic Symphony. I follow the notes on the page closely, practicing Shostakovich's happy folk dances, then Prokofiev's upbeat marches, then Igor Stravinsky's more disciplined, staccato *Symphonies of the Wind Instruments*. My fingers move rapidly among the rings; my breath blows steadily into the mouthpiece. With all this focus on the music, I find that I can escape into the melodies in the same way I escape into run-ning and the little piece of light in Roy's closet. When I'm playing music, I can forget my life.

In the fall semester of seventh grade, my music teacher praises my skill and invites me to join the school band. I'm unsure of whether my mother will let me participate in an extracurricular activity. When I ask her, she says, "Perhaps it could promote your potential for university scholarships."

On afternoons when I'm not practicing the clarinet in the school's music room, I continue to spend afternoons locked out of our apartment. "May I please get a key?" I ask Mother, time and again. "I don't have anywhere to go after school." Mother finally tells Roy it's OK to arrange for me to have a babysitter in the afternoons. Roy sets this up, hiring an older woman, a mother of grown children, who lives nearby. I've seen her inside our apartment on occasion speaking alone with Roy.

One afternoon a few weeks after she's started babysitting me, I'm watching *Magilla Gorilla* on her sofa. She comes and sits down next to me and begins to chat with me about school, my homework, whether I like the TV show. She puts her arms around me and I hug her back, loving the warmth of this scarce embrace.

The next thing I know, her hand is on my breast. "You're beautiful," she whispers. She begins to caress me, and I'm instantly frozen. It feels like my stomach has dropped through the floor; I'm so devastated I think I might throw up.

She lifts up my shirt and begins sucking my breasts, and then she puts her hand between my legs.

I don't know how to ask for a key from Mother again without getting in trouble.

The next day after school, I sit silently on the edge of the babysitter's sofa and watch TV. She picks up on my discomfort and leaves me alone, but it won't be the last time she touches me. A couple of weeks later, Roy comes to her apartment to take me home, and the two of them make small talk before he takes a seat on her sofa while I'm sitting in the chair next to it, waiting for him to say it's time to go home. Instead, I watch as the babysitter sits down right next to him, and the two of them begin to kiss. I drop my eyes, horrified again. They rub each other, and from the way they touch, it's clear to me that they've carried on like this together before. For a moment, Roy turns and looks at me. I know I have to do what they want, or it will be my fault and I'll be in trouble. Life in the apartment could turn from uncomfortable to very violent.

I search my mind, trying to understand how someone as sharp as my adoptive mother, who has made a career of studying mental health and understanding patterns of behavior, doesn't know that something's happening whenever she's not home. Even if her intuition isn't enough to suggest that strange things are going on, doesn't she find things rumpled or out of place in the closet? Doesn't she wonder what the neighbors say about Roy and his odd business operations in our apartment?

However, I'm aware there are two sides to my mother: the sometimes-attentive side she allows me to see inside our apartment, and the proud, intellectual side that she wants people outside to see. Anytime we're doing an errand in the neighborhood, she keeps her chin held high and refuses to make eye contact with any deli worker or cashier who waits on her. She doesn't speak warmly with the women who live in our building or on our block. On the infrequent occasion they stop her to speak, she stares down the straightness of her nose at them and responds with brisk answers. As I keep up alongside her on the sidewalk, I'm the only one to whom Mother speaks. She tells me about her many accomplishments, the fact that she's a member of Mensa, the international society for people with high IQs. She continues to advance her degrees and receive promotions at her job, she says, and she works out of a number of state offices around the city. Downtown, in the World Trade Center, her office is on the very same floor as the governor's office. I can see she's pleased to maintain her image as the neighborhood genius—for her, intelligence and image are everything.

By now, I'm only eleven years old, but as Roy shares information about small pieces of their life with me, the more I understand the two of them as individuals. As much as I ache to be loved as someone's child, the truth in all this is that we are not a family. They are not my parents. The two of them share a bedroom but live very separate lives, and Roy begins to see me as his live-in child mistress. "If I were younger, things would be different," he tells me one day. "You'd be my wife. Then I wouldn't have to put up with her and all those books." Everything he says to me, everything he does, creates a complex struggle inside of me. The result is that even as the child in this, I blame myself for all of it. "No one will ever love you the way I do," he says.

I raise my eyes from the ground to look up at him. In the silence of my heart, I can't understand what I did to deserve this confused kind of love.

Inside the closet with him, I decide that little piece of light coming in from under the door means hope and possibility. It means that beyond the dark, dangerous closet, there is light somewhere else—and one day, I can get to it. It means that I have a light inside myself that Roy can't touch or put out no matter what he does. I focus on that sliver of light until I disappear into it and feel nothing and nowhere—least of all, in this closet.

Each night, when Mother returns home from work, Roy is down the hall working with leather or playing his acoustic guitar. "What points have you earned today, Donna Patricia?" Mother asks me, as she sets her bags onto the floor and unwinds a scarf from her neck.

"I've done all my homework," I tell her.

"Excellent. And?"

"I practiced the clarinet."

"What else?"

Actually, there is another accomplishment that I'd like to share with her: the track and field coach at school has asked me to join the school team. One morning during phys ed class, Miss Berry approached me. "I think you'd make a great competitor," she said. "Would you like to join the team?"

Maybe, I told her, but I probably wouldn't be allowed.

"I'll speak to your parents anytime they'd like," Miss Berry said. "You have talent that shouldn't go to waste."

"I should say, I don't quite see the point in all that," Mother says when I ask her. "I'd sooner see you focus on your academics. It's brains that really get a young woman places, you know."

It's my running that could really get me places, I want to tell her. *Maybe even away from here.*

When I share my mother's decision with Miss Berry, she calls

Mother and makes the case that my running has the potential to get me into top universities when the time comes.

"What kind of equipment would be necessary for us to purchase for Donna?" Mother asks her.

"Not a thing," Miss Berry tells her. "The school will supply everything she needs."

That's when Mother finally relents. Miss Berry gives me a school uniform and running shoes, and she eyes her stopwatch closely while I run. I sprint so hard, so fast, that within days I'm crossing the finish line before the rest of the team. "Give us one of those magic runs of yours," Miss Berry always tells me.

Magic. The second my toe touches the start line, I'm above my body, soaring direct as a hummingbird.

When my name begins to appear in local newspapers for beating runners in my district, Mother and Roy still don't budge from the bedroom to appear at my meets. At night, Miss Berry drops me off outside our building, and I creep into the dim apartment and down the hall slowly to find the two of them sitting up in bed. Roy makes a concentrated effort to keep his eyes on the television, while Mother glances up at me over her glasses as she holds an open book against her ribs. "Well?" she asks. "How did it go?"

"I came in first."

She raises her eyebrows and lowers her eyes back to her book. "Well done," she says.

I wait for the night when she'll rise out of bed, hug me, kiss my head…and tell me she's proud of me. *Good job, Donna Patricia.* These four words are all I want. Instead, from behind her book she says, "The program you like is on." I lean against their bedroom doorway, watching *Within These Walls* about a prison full of female inmates who are trying to survive after being punished, often unfairly, for crimes they committed, sometimes unknowingly. *How can they live like that?* I wonder. I'm hooked on this show because I believe the way the women overcome their struggles might reveal answers for how I could overcome being trapped inside this home.

"Would you bring in the tea, please?" Mother asks me. I pull my interest from *Within These Walls* to turn and walk slowly toward the kitchen. I feel lonely, abandoned, just like the characters on the show. I wish for my mother's love…for her encouragement…

And I wish most of all for a lock on my bedroom door.

In the evenings, Roy makes a plate of food and takes his dinner into their bedroom. With me at the dining room table, Daphne eats hurriedly before wiping the edges of her mouth and dropping her napkin on her plate to return to her work. "When you're through cleaning up the kitchen," she asks me, "would you please prepare the tea?"

As I finish my plate, my only company is the clink of my silverware against china, the ticking of the clock on the kitchen wall. One night, I can no longer take the loneliness of living in their home for each of them to use me to get what they both need. As I crouch under the sink to search for the dish soap, I spot a box of boric acid with a cartoon image of a dead mouse on it. I stretch my neck to listen for any footsteps approaching, and then I spill a spoonful of rat poison into each cup. I pour the tea and let it steep, stirring in extra sugar to cover up the taste of the poison.

I start down the hallway and walk into their bedroom. Both of them sit up, preparing to take the cups from my hands. Suddenly, I stop in my tracks. I spin around and head back for the kitchen.

I can't do it.

"Donna Patricia!" Daphne calls after me. "What are you doing?"

"I made it wrong!" I call over my shoulder. I pour the tea down the drain. As I splash water from the spigot around the sink, I feel sick. I can't believe I even attempted it. *See, Donna?* I tell myself. *You're bad. You deserve everything that's happening to you.*

No matter how much my adoptive parents have hurt me, I can't hurt them. At twelve years old, I know that I'm not someone who can harm someone else. I take two clean cups from the cupboard and prepare another pot of tea.

2

GOLDEN CHILD

Inside the closet, I continue to focus on the light that streams beneath the door each day. When I try to resist Roy's beckoning toward the closet, he begins to threaten me with scissors and knives, just as I saw him do to my mother right after they first brought me here. He's begun to hold me against the wall and put his hand on my throat to the point where I can't breathe.

Staying away from home is my main motivator to train so obsessively. Out on the track, I'm not someone's servant. Here, I am *someone*.

In seventh grade, I win district-wide running competitions. In the fall of eighth grade, Miss Berry names me captain of the team, with a girl called Nancy my co-captain. Physically, we are opposites: Nancy is short and muscular, while my limbs are long and lean. What we share in common, however, is that we are both reserved until the stopwatch starts. There's something about competing against one another that brings out a respect between the two of us. No matter what emotional struggle I may be dealing with, my finish time is always an objective fact. Nancy and I always know where we stand with each other, and even though we're competitors, we both acknowledge that we're on the same team. Nancy and Miss Berry are the only two people in my life I can trust.

As co-captains, we run against other New York City students at various meets around the city. A big opportunity comes when we both qualify to compete in a meet to be held at Madison Square Garden. I come in first, and a small local newspaper calls me "the fastest girl in the Bronx." Nancy is always gracious, cheering me on with high fives and encouragement.

At practice, the whole team screams for me as Miss Berry watches the clock. *"Gogogogogogogogo,"* she says as I blow past her, doubling over at the finish line to catch my breath. Then I stand tall and clasp my fingers behind my head, victorious. Running is the single thing in my life that makes me feel powerful when, at home, I'm nothing more than that helpless child inside Roy's closet.

With Nancy, I earn a spot to compete at Brooklyn's Pratt Institute in the prestigious Colgate Games, the nation's largest track competition for young girls. "This race will be big, Donna," says Miss Berry. "You've got to place first or second. People are looking at you. Do you think you'd want to be in the Olympics?"

"The Olympics?" I let this sink in. "Are you serious, Miss Berry?"

"Very serious. Olympics scouts have their eyes on you. If you want to go, then we have to get serious about your training. We'd have to enter you through track and field, and you've got to start training on the hurdles."

"I'll do it," I tell her, accepting any chance to stay out of the house. These hurdles will be nothing compared to what I'm living there.

Every day, I devote myself to training and practice on the hurdles, knowing that running could quite literally be my real escape from my life at home. But it's around this time when during the day, I begin to see shadowy figures leap out in front of me. I jump back, trying to fight and push them off. "Donna?" Miss Berry asks me on the track one afternoon. "Are you OK?"

"I'm fine," I assure her. If there's anyone in the world whose confidence I need, it's Miss Berry's. However, the situation reaches a critical point the night before the semifinals. I'm running to represent our entire district, and Miss Berry says a lot of good scouts will be there. I *have* to win this. The night before the meet, my duffel bag is already packed with my uniform and sneakers and sitting next to my bedroom door, waiting for morning to arrive. But late that night, Miss Berry calls with the worst possible news. "I'm terribly sick with the flu," she tells my mother. "Please tell Donna I'm so sorry I can't take her to the meet."

Mother comes into my bedroom and shrugs coolly. "I'm sorry, Donna Patricia," she says. "Miss Berry promised us that she would be your ride anytime you had a meet."

In despair, I ask her: "Will you take me, just this one time?"

"Absolutely not," she says. "And neither will your father. The agreement was that if you want to run, your ride wouldn't be our responsibility."

This race is everything to me. It's not often I show emotion in front of Roy and my mother, but here, I begin to cry. I beg them. This means everything to me, and it wounds me so deeply that Roy can hurt me the way that he does and not even take this one opportunity to help me in the way that matters most in my life. Their lack of support crushes me more than anything I've ever experienced. Running is the only thing that makes me feel normal. This is my proudest accomplishment.

When I don't show up for the race, we lose by forfeit.

The shadows continue to jump out at me in the daylight. At night, I jolt awake from dreams where Roy is standing next to my bed, staring at me while I sleep. After school, I try to take my time getting home…but that doesn't stop Roy from summoning me into the closet before he hears Mother's key inside the front door.

We must learn to find our own solutions. I continue to search for answers or some way out, often sliding the Bible off the book-shelves to seek some comfort in God's word. Not even that can make sense of what I've experienced every day for the past three years. I can't find the answer in the Bible or anywhere else, so I go to the only other place I can possibly think of: the school coun-selor's office. I knock on her door, hoping I can find the solution here. "Can I help you?" she says.

"May I please speak with you?"

"You may," she says. "Is it a private matter?"

I nod, unable to look her in the eyes.

"You can close the door," she says. "Have a seat."

I slide myself tentatively into the wooden chair across from her desk and look down at my hands to share with her: "I need help."

"What's wrong?"

"I can't take it anymore."

"What can't you take?"

"My father keeps hurting me."

"I'm sorry, Donna...I'm not sure I understand."

"He takes me into the closet," I tell her, "and I don't know what to do."

"Does your mother know this is happening?"

I shake my head. *No.* "I don't know how to tell her." The real truth that pulses inside me is that I'm the one to blame.

"Would you like me to call your mother and tell her all this?"

I nod. If Mother will just let me have a lock on my bedroom door, I could lock him out and stay there peacefully for the next few years, until I'm old enough to live somewhere else.

The counselor slides open a heavy metal file drawer and pulls out my file with a gesture of great purpose. She picks up her telephone and begins to put in a number, each spin of the rotary dial holding my full attention. I sit upright and stare at the square white tiles in the ceiling, on edge, but hopeful. I know that this singular moment could change everything—I only hope it will be for the better.

The guidance office is so still that I can hear the other line ringing through the counselor's earpiece. I stay calm, but am filled with tension. After a few seconds, I realize that I need to remind myself to breathe.

"Mrs. Hylton?" says the counselor. "I have your daughter here in my office. She's shared some information with me that I think you should know about. Right—she says her father's been hurting her." I watch her side of the conversation carefully. "That's correct, it seems he's touching her inside the closet?" She goes silent for a moment, nodding along to the other side of the dialogue. "Mm-hm. Mm-hm. OK." She holds the phone out to me. "Your mother would like a word with you."

She's finally going to hear me and allow me to have a lock on my bedroom door. "Yes?" I say into the phone.

Donna Patricia! I startle at the screech of my mother's voice in my ear. "Why are you making up these lies?"

"I'm not lying!" My conviction comes out strongly at first.

"How dare you? Why would you make up these stories?"

By now, I've crumpled in the seat, hope quickly deflating. "But I'm not lying."

"You know what happens to people who lie?" she says. "They get caught, and they spend their lives in prison just like those women you watch on that television program!"

I'm telling the truth! I want to tell her. *You must know this is happening!*

"You listen to me," she continues. "If your father finds out what you've done, you know he's going to be very angry."

Immediately, I know she's right. My face caves into silent tears. All of my courage has disintegrated in an instant and suddenly I'm ill with fear.

"Donna Patricia, are you there?"

"Yes," I whisper.

"Pardon me?"

"Yes," I force with my only remaining strength.

"What do you have to say for yourself?"

I say the only thing I can think of: "I'm sorry." With these two words, I've given in. *I'm wrong. I'm the one who's bad.*

My wrist is limp when I hand the phone back to the guidance counselor. "Is everything OK now?" she says.

Disillusioned and now with no one to turn to, I tell her, "Yes."

I hadn't considered this outcome even as a possibility: neither the counselor nor my mother will believe me. Dazed and nauseated with pain, I walk alone to the restroom outside the gymnasium, which is the only place I feel safe and familiar enough to let it out. *"Help me!"* I scream. *"HELP ME!"*

Standing over the sink, I look in the mirror...and I see Roy's face. "No!" I cry. *"LEAVE ME ALONE!"* I turn to the window, but also there his face peers back at me. A burst of raging pain comes out of me, and I cry out.

Suddenly I look down, and there's shattered glass around my tennis shoes and blood dripping from my right hand. I look back up at the window, where Roy's face had just been, and I can only add the details together: I've punched my hand through the window and sliced a piece of my flesh off my wrist. I place my hand under the sink to rinse the blood with cold water, then hurry to wrap tissue and paper towels to make a bandage for my arm. I kneel quickly, focusing through my tears to pick up the shards of glass that fell on the floor.

Then I rush out of the school's side entrance. When I arrive at home, Roy waits at the door. "How dare you?" he snarls in my face. "I told you that no one would believe you! What are you trying to do, mess up stuff between me and my wife?"

I cruise past him toward my bedroom, taking a seat on my bed to try to figure out what to do. I'm playing a clarinet solo in the school band concert tonight. My mind races as I try to work out how I'll change clothes to be ready in time.

Just then Roy blasts into my room and squeezes his hands around my throat. Choking, unable to breathe, I try to rip his hands off of me until two of my fingernails manage to scratch his face. He rocks back in shock. "You made me bleed, you little bitch!" He stares at the blood on his hands, then goes into his bedroom and slams the door.

Likewise, I rise and close my bedroom door, even though he doesn't allow it. I look outside, the late summer sun still blazing hot. Even though the rest of the kids in the school band will wear their short sleeves with our uniform at the concert tonight, I choose the long-sleeved shirt to hide the cut on my wrist. I know that I'll look different from everyone else. I *am* different from everyone else. It's as though today's events give me no choice but to live with this.

When Mother arrives at home, my bedroom door bursts open like thunder. "Are we clear?" she says. "Do you understand what I said to you earlier?"

Accepting the blame, I don't look at her.

"Did you hear me?"

Still unable to make eye contact, I nod.

"I never want to have another phone call like that, Donna Patricia. And aren't you expected to play your clarinet tonight? Come on," she says. "I'll take you." Her offer to accompany me is not proper parenting. It's damage control to assure I don't spout off to anyone what's happening at home.

I play my clarinet in formation with the band, always the dutiful schoolgirl doing what is expected. But far beneath the cut on my skin, I am so deeply wounded. Locking my lips around the mouthpiece of the clarinet strengthens me not to cry. My adoptive parents won't listen to me, and neither will the school counselor, but in the concert audience there's a sea of faces I don't know. Aware that Mother must be sitting somewhere out there, I sit up straight in my chair when my solo arrives. I play the music with more concentrated focus than I ever have in my life. When the song reaches its final note, the audience breaks into applause. I imagine that they're cheering for me, cheering to have just heard what's inside of me.

In the second half of eighth grade, my classmates and I take the Secondary School Admission Test, known familiarly in New York City as the SSAT. The scores from this standardized test rank students' academic performance in comparison to one another and give administrators at the city's public and private high schools a basis for accepting applicants. Students who rank relatively high gain admission into the city's best public schools, such as the Bronx High School of Science, from which students often graduate to attend top-tier universities.

When the test scores come in several weeks after we take the exams, I learn that my scores have ranked me third among all the eighth graders in New York City. With this score, along with my performance as a runner, I receive notification that I've won a scholarship to St. Andrew's School in Delaware, a prestigious boarding school with fewer than seventy-five students per class. The brochures for St. Andrew's show a green campus that sits on the edge of a lake with grand brick architecture, bright classrooms, expansive fields for sports, and an auditorium for theater productions and music recitals. As many of my teachers react to the news of my acceptance, I quickly come to understand that St. Andrew's is one of the best private high schools in the entire country. My music teacher praises me, telling me that with scores like this, I could have my pick of Harvard, Yale, Princeton, or Brown when it comes time to apply for college.

I receive an award from the mayor of New York City and from my school district. At home, my scholarship to St. Andrew's is the one thing that has smoothed over my talk with the school counselor. Mother begins to tout my acceptance to her colleagues at work, who congratulate me with gifts of money, which begin to arrive in the mail. Mother delightfully keeps the funds in a neat white envelope in her bedroom. It seems as though she tallies each one as another pat on her own back for having raised me so well.

I stand tall in her presence. *I've made her happy.* I hope that because I've achieved what she wanted, she'll finally begin to see that I'm just like other kids—that I'm good enough. I'm the clone she's spent the past seven years molding me to be. I seek a touch, a word, a sound, a hug, some stroke of tangible love from her. Instead, as my eighth grade school year winds down, she says, "I still fear you're going to be different from the other students at St. Andrew's, you know."

My scores on the SSAT prove that I'm every bit as good as the other students...but with every tutorial and critique from her, my goodness matters less. A New York newspaper even writes an article about me, referring to me as "the Golden Child." But I don't feel golden. I feel like garbage—like nothing. No matter what I accomplish, in the eyes of my mother, I'll never be worthy of love or praise.

She schedules a meeting with my math teacher, Mr. Harris. I sit in on their discussion, where Mother tells Mr. Harris that it would be beneficial to my time at St. Andrew's if he will tutor me over the summer in advanced mathematics. "I work with her in writing and comprehension," Mother tells Mr. Harris, "but it's of utmost importance that Donna is up to par with her peers in calculus and trigonometry."

"My wife and I just had a baby," Mr. Harris says. "If Donna will babysit for us during the summer, I can spend some time tutoring her."

He and Mother arrange for me to stay for several nights each week at his house. I dutifully do my laundry and pack my duffel bag, eager to spend most of my summer without the daily threat of danger and Roy's leering. In early June, when Mr. Harris drives me outside of the city to his house in suburban New Jersey, I discover a landscaped wonderland. Decorating each green yard are trees and flowers, like the homes of the families on TV shows. Inside Mr. Harris's house is something I've never seen before: carpeting. Everything about the home feels soft and comfortable, like family.

Mr. Harris's wife is cheerful and pretty, holding the baby as she takes a break from stirring dinner on the stove to welcome me. She shows me to their guest bedroom, where I instinctively notice that there's a push lock on the inside of the door. When they go out for groceries, my toes make impressions in the carpet as I peek gently around the rooms, trying to absorb this feeling. *What is home?* I remember asking Roy when I first arrived in New York.

This is home.

I take immediately to their adorable infant son, and help Mrs. Harris with things around the house or answer the phone while her hands are full with the baby. In the afternoons, I sit on the edge of their community swimming pool and watch Mrs. Harris swish the baby's torso in the shallow end. I see the love in their faces when Mrs. Harris holds him in the air while they make big smiles and squeals at each other. There's a pang in my stomach as a memory of my mother in Jamaica bursts into my mind. *Ooh, I love you,* she'd say with a hug. Suddenly, I miss her terribly. "You're never going to leave Mommy and Daddy, are you, darling?" Mrs. Harris says. The baby rests his sweet temple against his mother's collarbone, as if to agree to the promise. Their closeness twists my heart in longing. *I wish I had a mother who loved me too much to ever let me go.*

A few weeks later, in mid-July, I stay at their house while Mr. Harris takes his wife and baby out to visit relatives. They plan to take me out for pizza when they get back. As I draw a bath to rinse off the swimming pool's chlorine from earlier in the day, the phone rings, and I turn off the bath water to run to the kitchen and answer it. "My wife and son aren't coming home yet," Mr. Harris tells me, "but I'll still take you to dinner."

I return to the bathroom, putting on only my bra and underwear to stay cool while I blow out my hair, section by section with a brush, instead of braiding it like a child, the way Mother always insists. When I turn the hair dryer off to crack the door open for air, I'm startled to hear a little tap on the door. "It's me," Mr. Harris says. "I'm home."

I stand away from the door's opening. "I'm getting ready!"

"Take your time," he says. "Did you think about where you want to go to eat?"

"It doesn't matter!" I'm trying to cower with my hands close to my chest, the hair dryer and the brush guarding my body.

"I'll let you finish."

Believing he's walked away, I push the door nearly closed so that he can't see in. I turn the hair dryer back on and wrap a towel tighter around me until I can get to my clothes in the bedroom where I stay. *My hair's good enough,* I think. *Let me hurry up.*

But then, the door opens. Mr. Harris stands still for a moment and then walks toward me as I freeze in place. The feel of his golf shirt against my bare back causes a thousand needles to rise up in alarm under my skin. *This isn't right!*

In the mirror, he makes eye contact with me. "You're so pretty," he says.

No. No. Not Mr. Harris. In my experience of this, it's always

46

begun with a flattering reference to my appearance. I can never hear this as a genuine compliment, but rather as a stated intent to take advantage of me.

Mr. Harris kisses on my neck, then my shoulder. I search for something to focus on, the way I do with the little piece of light inside Roy's closet. When I can't find something, I rise up out of my body and dissociate.

When I come to, I'm in Mr. Harris's bed. I don't know how much time has passed, how I got here, or what has happened. When I jerk my head to get my bearings, he's lying beside me. This man has been one of the best teachers I've ever had, the only man I've ever been able to trust. What is his wife going to say?

This is my fault.

"Come on," he says. "I don't know when she'll be home."

When Mrs. Harris arrives at home, I won't allow my eyes to meet her face. Everything that I wanted to believe about their family has been shattered. I've wanted a mother just like her. I wanted to believe that one day, I could have a life like hers. Mr. Harris has betrayed her, and he's betrayed *me* . . . still, I'm the one who did this.

A few days later, back in Boynton, I exit my bedroom to see a man leaving the apartment. "I'll see about the paperwork," Roy tells him. "Come by tomorrow."

When the man returns the next day, he and Roy go on the terrace to talk. *I want to go out there,* I think, but I don't want to impose on two adults in conversation. When Roy breaks from their conversation to walk inside, I step onto the terrace. I don't know this man's name, but I recognize him from one of the apartments upstairs where he lives with his mother.

"What's your name?" he asks me.

I stare at the ground. "My name is Donna."

"Donna, my name's Alvin. I heard you had a scholarship."

"Yes," I tell him, now slowly meeting his eyes. *How did you hear?* "I have a scholarship."

"I hear you're good in school." This feels good—that he recognizes me. Roy returns, and Alvin meets him in the living room to finish their conversation.

When I see Alvin the next day, he asks me, "Hey…are you OK?"

I look down. "Yeah."

"Are you sure? I'm your friend, you know. You can tell me anything. If something's wrong, I won't tell anyone." I want to trust him, but after what happened with Mr. Harris, I don't know if I can believe anyone anymore. He asks me again: "Are you OK?"

With this prompt, my will to hide the truth collapses. "No," I tell him. "I have to get away from here."

"But your scholarship—"

"I'm tired of him touching me!"

Alvin watches me in silence. "What do you mean he's touching you?"

I stop myself. *I shouldn't say any more.*

Roy enters the room and Alvin keeps his eye on me as the two of them speak. Before Alvin leaves, he turns around. "Remember what I told you," he tells me. "You take care of yourself. OK?" I look at Roy, who's carefully reading our interaction.

"OK," I tell Alvin.

Roy says nothing when I return to Mr. Harris's once again, feeling doomed for more abuse. Mr. Harris treats me normally in front of his wife, and he is surprisingly mindful not to cross the line or make another advance toward me. When I return to Boynton a few days later, I find not Roy in our apartment but Alvin. "Your father's gone out to get something," he says. "He should be back soon. Hey—how are you doing?" Tears spring to my eyes. "What's wrong?" Alvin says.

"I want to go away," I whisper. "I don't want to be here anymore."

"I'll take you away," Alvin says. "I'll help you. Tell me everything."

I start to tell him what Roy's been doing, this time in greater detail. I tell him what my teacher did, and how I'm not sure if I can stand any of it even for another day. No matter where I turn for help or an escape, I can't find anyone to trust.

"I promise that I'm going to take you away so no one else can hurt you," Alvin says. "I'll protect you. Do you want to go away to school? Or do you want me to help you now?"

After what's happened with Mr. Harris, I don't know what to expect from school anymore. Alvin's offer of protection sounds real in this moment—better than any alternative. *This is what I've got to do.* "I want you to help me now."

"OK."

"When I got the scholarship," I tell him, tears dropping down my cheeks, "everyone was so happy. I felt like I did something right."

"I know," he says. "I've read about you. How much money do you have?"

I shrug. "I think about three hundred dollars."

"We'll need that to run away," he says. "Save up what you can for the next week or two. Then the night before we leave, you'll have to pack. Otherwise, act the same as you usually do. You don't want to alert anyone that I'm taking you away to protect you." He shows me how to turn the lock on our apartment door to make it appear locked, when it's not really. Late at night when Roy and Mother are in bed, I practice and practice this until I have it down.

Two weeks later, I slide the envelope from the spot where Mother has kept track of my school money. I wash my clothes and repack my suitcase, just as I do anytime I go to Mr. Harris's. But this time—Wednesday night, August 1, 1979—I do one small thing differently: I place my bag on a chair by the apartment door. Convinced I'm just preparing to leave the following morning to babysit, neither of my parents questions it.

At 10:30 p.m. when the apartment is silent with sleep, I slink out of bed and dress myself quickly. I hold my breath with every move, listening for any sign of stirring or suspicion. There's nothing.

What if this is a bad idea? I think. *I don't have to go.* But it's my faith in Alvin's promise to not let anyone else hurt me that gives me the courage to grab my suitcase and go meet him at the spot he designated, in the back of the building at a dark area next to the parking lot.

Outside, I can't tell if my fear is magnifying how eerie the quiet is. When I reach our spot, Alvin's silhouette stands waiting for me. "Did anyone hear you?"

I shake my head no. "No one heard me."

"Do you have the money?"

I hand him the envelope.

"Come on," he says, and we rush around the corner of the building, onto the sidewalk, and into the night.

"Where are we going?"

"To the Port Authority."

"Why?"

"Because we have to leave town. If we stay in New York, they'll find us, and I won't be able to protect you."

We walk to the train station and drop our tokens in the slot to board the number five train headed to Manhattan. On the train, a guy carrying a boombox is playing a song that I recognize:

Ain't no stopping us now!
We're on the move!

My head bounces with the beat, and suddenly, I'm filled with courage.

It's close to midnight when we arrive at the Port Authority. Alvin walks to a board that lists the cities the Greyhound bus travels to. "Where do you want to go?" he asks.

I stand before the board, daunted. "I have no idea."

"Close your eyes and point your finger," he says, "and walk to the board. Wherever your finger lands, that's where we'll go." I close my eyes and do as he says, our fate relying on my random tactile guess. "Walk," he tells me. "Now open them." When I do, my finger is pressed over Philadelphia. "Looks like we're going to Philly," he says. "Do you have an ID?"

"No."

"You don't have a birth certificate?"

"No. I have citizenship papers, but my mother keeps them."

"Here, take this." He gives me an ID card with his mother's photograph on it. "If anyone asks, this is your name and you're nineteen years old." I look at the image of Alvin's mother, a woman with graceful, tired eyes. *Something about this doesn't feel right.* "Don't worry," he says, as if in response to my thoughts. "You'll be fine with me."

One hour later, we're on a bus headed ninety minutes west, to Philadelphia. My stomach has butterflies and every part of me is shaking, but I can't tell whether I'm afraid, unsure, or even maybe a little excited. My face feels heavy with exhaustion, but adrenaline courses through me. *I shouldn't be doing this. Will my mother be angry? Will my father come at me again? Alvin has to protect me now.* We arrive in Philadelphia to an early morning that's just as muggy and serene as the city we've just left. Alvin locates a motel near the bus terminal, and I stand by at the check-in desk while he reserves a room with the money from my envelope. *But—why is he only getting one room?*

When he unlocks the motel room door and flips on the light, my stomach flutters so severely that I think I might faint. I refuse to cross the threshold to join him in the room: it has two dim bedside lamps, a TV, a bathroom . . . and one bed.

Seeing my hesitation, Alvin says, "We have to hold on to the money. Don't worry, we're just going to rest. It's OK." The feeling in my stomach swells even harder than before, but I don't argue. I've never run away before; I don't know how this works. I don't even really know how to use money. *Maybe I should hurry up and get back home before they realize I left,* I think, quickly weighing it. *I'm going to be in so much trouble when they find out that I tried to run away.*

"Calm down," Alvin assures me. "Right now we'll rest. Then tomorrow, we'll figure out what to do."

His words soothe my nerves only a little while a feeling inside seems to warn me that something is very wrong. I'm fourteen years old, alone in a motel room in a strange city with a man who's ten years older than I am. The pieces of this equation somehow don't add up to safety and protection. But, this was my only hope. I've trusted Alvin all along up to now, but I start to weigh out how I might be able to defend myself. He's the same height as me, but he's broader. In a physical fight, we might be a match, but I've already seen that he has a lot of confidence in himself . . . and by now I certainly know that when a man really wants something from me, there's not much I can do to make him stop.

Alvin begins to take off his clothes. "Get ready for bed," he instructs me. "We have to make sure they're not looking for you."

I enter the bathroom to change as he directed, then I brush my teeth. I also wash up and put on a clean pair of panties and bra under my nightgown, as Mother has taught me. When I step out of the bathroom and stand at the foot of the bed, there's a smile on Alvin's face. "Get in," he tells me.

I approach the bed slowly. As I get in and begin to situate myself under the covers, he says, "Take the nightgown off."

I pause, motionless. "Take my nightgown off?"

"Yeah. Why do you need to wear all that to bed?"

"Because *I'm going to bed.*"

"Take off the nightgown." He begins to pull it over my head. My ears blaze hot with the alarm in my head, but not knowing what else to do, I slowly lie down. Alvin cups his elbow around my head on the pillow, and says, "You're beautiful."

No. I feel trapped—even more trapped than I did at home, or with Mr. Harris. I'm in a different state with someone I don't know, so far from home. There's nothing I can do. This time, I lose.

"Don't worry," he whispers. "I'll take care of you. I'm going to love you."

This takes me back to what Roy always tells me: *No one will ever love you the way I do.*

Now Alvin unhooks my bra—*No, please no*—and starts to rub and kiss on my breasts. I start to feel myself drift…drift… drift…I'm back in Jamaica…walking by the water…running… laughing…looking for seashells…

I know that Alvin has taken my clothes off, but I can't actually sense it—until I hear his jeans unzip while he climbs on top of me. Then I feel pain. I *scream*! Even Roy has never invaded me as harshly as this. Whatever part of me wasn't broken is broken now. I'm ripped open in a way that I've never been before.

After he finishes, Alvin rolls aside. I breathe shallowly, tears dropping silently down my temple, dampening the edge of my hair. When his breathing has grown calm and steady in sleep, I move carefully out of the bed and click the bathroom door closed quietly behind me before I turn on the light and lock the door. When I sit on the toilet to let my body flush out what Alvin's done to me, there is fresh blood on my panties. This never happened with Roy, who was not as violent and forceful as Alvin just was. I realize for the first time that my adoptive father could never remain hard for as long as this pain just lasted.

Please, I beg in my mind, looking up at the brown water stain on the motel bathroom's ceiling. *Please find me.*

For a week, we move from motel to motel, the murmurs of cocaine deals happening outside our door at almost every one. The rapes continue every single day, sometimes multiple times a day, and they grow progressively worse in severity.

Within a week, my money envelope has grown thin. Alvin is no longer the man I looked to, to rescue me. I am more lost in my life than I've ever been before. I'm a little girl, trying to navigate alone in the world with a grown man telling me what to do. I have nowhere to go; I have no one—here or anywhere. I cannot believe that I risked my chance to go away to St. Andrew's for this.

When our money runs out, our next move is as unclear as the misty evening rain that's falling on us in William Penn Park—a place where at least I feel safe from the rape. I eat a soft pretzel from a park vendor, the first I've eaten all day. "This is a pretty park," I say.

"This is where we'll sleep tonight."

"What do you mean?"

"We're running out of money," he says. "Don't worry. This is what people do when they're in love."

Mother has told me that homeless people are all derelicts of society, useless human beings who are strung out on heroin.

I want to go home.

The next day, we walk into a parking garage that sits beneath a fancy apartment building. Alvin puffs out his chest and approaches the manager, while the two of them engage in a brief exchange. The manager looks at me skeptically, but moments later, Alvin jogs back toward me. "You're welcome," he says.

"Why?"

"Because I just got us a job parking cars."

"I can't drive a car!"

"Yes you can," he says. "Remember? You're nineteen."

Each night after the other workers leave, Alvin and I slide into the backseat of a customer's vehicle, where we sleep for a few hours until it's time to open the garage entrance. In the morning, the manager puts me in the cashier booth handling the tickets and the customers' money, and I occasionally park a few cars when the guys all have their hands full. Behind the wheel of the residents' cars, I wind slowly and cautiously around each bend in the garage, holding my breath until the vehicle is in Park. Believing that I'm perfectly capable of my responsibility for their vehicles, the customers pay me nice tips and converse with me. There's a particular older couple who make a point to bring me pieces of fruit or chocolate treats, which I eat quietly behind the talk-through glass of the attendant booth after they leave. One night when they return home from the opera, they give me their show program because I've told them I love opera and classical music.

I cling to these gentle acts of kindness, my only source of real refuge during what's becoming the most traumatic time of my life. The garage manager has a Doberman named Jaws, who becomes my companion, nuzzling against me on the days when Alvin's been the worst to me. "She never takes to strangers that way," the other garage attendants tell me. Intuitively Jaws seems to know that I'm hurting, in need of affection and protection.

After a week sleeping inside garage customers' cars, Alvin finds us a garden-level apartment in the back of a home in West Philadelphia. Inside there is no furniture, not a bed or sofa to sleep on; no pots or pans. "We'll fix it up later," he pledges. For weeks, we sleep curled on the floor, like Jaws does at the garage... but the way Alvin treats me here causes me to feel even lower than an animal. Sometimes, after he rapes me, he sits against the wall and orders me to crawl around the apartment on my hands and knees, like a dog. He stands up and urinates on my skin; he pushes the glowing tip of a cigarette against my bare leg. I survive all this by turning to the means I developed as a child: I drift out of my body and float upward, looking down at myself while he beats and humiliates me. Doing this keeps me detached, as if it's not happening to me—as if it's a horrible movie that I'm watching about someone else. It's my only way of escaping while I'm trapped with him here. Every day, I hope I'll be walking in Center City and someone will recognize the missing track star from the Bronx.

Please find me.

"You make me do these things to you!" Alvin says when he beats me. "I'm a man, and I do what I want." Other times, he tells me, "I do it because I love you."

Of course he must, because anyone who has ever loved me and promised to take care of me has hurt me in one way or another. His pledges of love confuse me in the same way Roy's did. *Please, someone, find me.*

In January 1980, after five months in Philadelphia, Alvin announces, "We need to go back. They're not looking for you anymore." In a car he borrows from the garage, Alvin drives us ninety minutes back to New York, where we stop at our old building in Boynton. While he's upstairs visiting his mother, I knock lightly, hesitantly, on my adoptive parents' door. I jump when Roy answers the door, staring me down for a moment and then moving aside in silence as my signal to enter. He and Mother say nothing as the three of us take awkward seats around the living room. They don't speak; they don't ask where I've been for the past five months, or with whom. All Mother says when she finally breaks the silence is: "I refuse to let you embarrass me."

I lower my eyes. She hasn't missed me, she hasn't worried, and as usual, her image in the community is more important than my well-being.

She stares at the floor in silence, which I take as a suggestion that she prefers I would leave. Their apartment door closes sternly behind me. Upstairs, where Alvin's mother, Dorothy, lives, I also sense her tension about my presence—she knows this relationship is not healthy, and she's determined to do something to end it once and for all. "Donna," Dorothy asks me, "would you still like to try to use your scholarship to go to school?"

"My scholarship?" I'd lost hope about going away to school when we ran away last August. "Do you think I still could?"

"I'll call St. Andrew's and find out," she says, but the admissions office informs her that they've given my scholarship away to another student. "If you'd called last week," the admissions director tells Dorothy, "we might have still been able to take Miss Hylton." I look at Alvin, who's playing with the dog that his mother looked after while we were in Philadelphia. *I've missed my chance by one week.*

Without school, I have no way out. Dorothy stands by in silence in the summertime of 1980, when Alvin moves us into an apartment in Harlem to be closer to the job Dorothy got him at the bank where she works. On weekends, he sings at a restaurant in our neighborhood with a disco and funk band. I begin working part-time as a waitress at the restaurant, always uncomfortable under Alvin's glare as I grow more familiar with the other staff, the regular neighborhood patrons, and the guys in the band. Alvin's typically careful never to hit me in the face, but after one August night when he catches me outside having a casual conversation with the band's lead singer, at home he unleashes the most horrible attack on me yet. The next day while he's at work, I leave his apartment and head directly to Boynton—the only place I can think to go. As I approach the lawn in front of our building, I bump into a neighbor who I knew from school. "Donna, are you alright?" she asks me. "I saw Alvin. He's looking for you."

"Please don't tell him I'm here!"

"You can stay with my family," she says, but in an instant I find myself on the ground, unable to breathe. As I fight back, Alvin wraps his hand around my throat to strangle me...and when he pulls up his other hand, he points a gun straight into my face. "Please," I gasp. "*No*—I'll do anything!" I stretch my neck enough to see that the neighbor girl has run off for her own safety. Minutes later, I'm next to Alvin on the train back down to Harlem.

This time I stay not so much because I care about my own life anymore; I stay because within a few weeks, I learn that I have another reason to stay alive—a reason that's truly worth living for.

For a few days after this episode with the gun, Alvin is calmer, which makes me feel a little less nervous to share with him that my breasts have begun to seep with fluid. "How do I go and see a doctor?" I ask him, trying to ease into the conversation in a way that won't set him off.

"What do you need to see any doctor for?"

"I think..." I'm aware there's no easy way to tell him this. "I think I might be pregnant."

His head cocks back, stunned at the news...and then he approaches me slowly. "Oh yeah?" he says. "No wonder you're pregnant, you're a *whore*!" He takes me by the wrists and knocks me down, holding me there while he forces himself on top of me. He enters me viciously and pumps himself inside of me so hard that I feel sick. "You tell me right now," he says, his breath heaving with each motion. I think I might vomit. "Was his dick bigger than mine? Huh? Was it? *WAS IT?*" he says as he thrusts himself into me. Then he slaps my face. "I'm a man!" he screams. *"I'M A MAN!"*

"No," I sob. "No, I promise. Please stop." He finishes with a grunt and collapses in exhaustion before he rises off of me. As he fastens his pants, he tells me: "That's not my baby, you slut."

There's no question that this is Alvin's baby... but what's more important is that this is *my* baby. Having a family has been my dream all my life: someone to need me, someone I can love and protect and care for. Disturbed by my news but trying to do the right thing in the face of a very compromised situation, Dorothy makes an appointment for me to see a doctor who confirms that I'm expecting a baby due in January. Alvin is agitated; Dorothy is concerned... but I have never been this happy. This child will be my light in the dark of winter, and for all the days of my life.

The pregnancy brings me to life, and I feel an unquestionable sense that she's a girl. Every day in the late summer after Alvin leaves for work, I exit the apartment and step out in the sun, walking one block south to Central Park, where I roam for hours and hours. As I wander, I place my hand on my belly, which is growing firmer and gradually rounder. I stretch headphones around the circumference of my midsection so that my child can learn to enjoy music as much as I do. All my life, I've longed for a companion. *I'm going to have somebody to love me*, I think, *and somebody I can love.* This baby will be my new light. Finally, I'll have something to live for.

I walk and walk and walk the park, for days and then weeks, already in love with this person who depends on the whole of my heart and my body to flourish. I encourage her growth, singing and praying and speaking to my child, resting from our walks only to fill us both with all the things I'm craving: cheesecake and ice cream sodas from diners on the Upper East Side, watermelon from the refrigerated cases of bodega stores on street corners. In every way, I will remember this as the sweetest, brightest time in my life.

"Oh my, Donna," says Dorothy as the chill of early fall moves in. "You're starting to show. We have to find some nicer clothes for you to wear, now that you're going to be a mother." For my sixteenth birthday, she helps me choose maternity shirts and comfortable pants, and a coat that will button around my belly in winter. My most reliable source of support, Dorothy also encourages me to sign up for my GED. I attend night classes to prepare for the test and pass in the fall with a very high score. Dorothy also makes an appointment for me at the hospital to learn the baby's gender. Sure enough, the doctor says, I'm having a little girl. *I knew it!*

When the snow begins to fall, it calls my attention inward. I tidy the apartment, clearing space in a closet and organizing drawers where the baby's clothes will go. I cook and clean and work every day to keep the cupboards neat so that when the baby comes, I can spend all my time with her. It appears that Alvin has begun to share my joy for what's coming, as well. As the baby moves actively inside me, his understanding changes of how this child came to be. "You're having my baby," he says, suddenly moved. I remember the name of a character I loved in a French novel I once read: Adrienne. Alvin agrees on the name, since it begins with the same letter as his own.

On February 3, 1981, Adrienne arrives—a full month after her due date. "Your life is going to be different than mine," I whisper as I cradle her in my arms. "I'm not going to let anything bad happen to you."

In the weeks to follow, I accept a bookkeeping job with our landlord to save up money so that I can make good on my solemn promise to Adrienne—*I'm not going to let anything bad happen to you.* With the baby here, Alvin's moods have turned more inconsistent and unpredictable than ever. "Shut that bitch up," he says when she cries in hunger, "before I do." I'm on edge anytime he goes near her, knowing that staying with him for very long will endanger my daughter's life.

One night he holds a kitchen knife to my face and threatens to kill me, and this is when I begin to plot our escape. In the middle of the night, under the cover of darkness, I flee with Adrienne and end up at the Hyltons' doorstep. "What are you doing here?" Roy asks me.

Unable to look at him, I confess: "I had nowhere else to go."

The next few months are a challenge as I try to be a mother, find a job, and straighten out my life. Even though Adrienne is a great light and a source of hope for me, I'm still mixed up and broken—still a child myself, with more terror in store.

What happens next unfolds over the course of a single week and leaves me so desperate and worn down that I'll do almost anything to lift myself up again.

One summer night as I'm exiting our building, a man jumps out from the bushes. I recognize him: he's an older man whom I've refused a few times when he's asked me to go out. Here in the falling dusk, he snatches me by the arm and shoves me inside a taxi, where he gives the cabbie a destination in Harlem. When we reach the projects where he lives, he locks me inside a bedroom closet and hands me a bucket. "Use that when you have to pee," he says, before he slams the closet door shut.

Every heartbeat inside me throbs with fear as I hear two men talking in the bedroom. I have to squint from the light as the closet door opens, where there stands a figure whose face and round stature I recognize: he's a minister at a nearby church. The minister grabs me, pushes me toward the bed, and climbs on top of me to hold me down as he undoes his pants. There, the two of them take turns raping me. Afterward, the first of the two shoves me back inside the closet, where I'll remain for three days until, finally, a woman discovers me while she's cleaning the house. "Get out!" she screams, and I take off, understanding that she's as horrified at the thought of my being held there as I have been.

When I return to the Bronx, a neighbor I knew from school notices how disheveled and distraught my appearance and demeanor are. "Donna," she says, "whatever happened, you need to talk to the police."

No. I've never approached anyone for help since the school counselor who brushed me aside four years ago, when I was twelve.

"Donna," she says, stepping in closer to me to ensure privacy in our conversation. "You don't have to tell me what happened to you, but you have to tell somebody. Come on. I'll go with you to the police."

After I give them my statement, the police converse for a moment. When their discussion breaks up, a detective tells my friend she can leave, that I have to go to the hospital for an examination. "I'll go along with her," says my friend.

"There's nothing you can do for her there," he says. "It's late. Go on home." Then the detective walks with me to an unmarked car and drives me to Jacobi Medical Center, where a doctor examines me for infections and a burn after one of the men singed the flesh on my leg with a cigarette lighter. With an ointment for the burn in hand, I exit the hospital and enter the detective's car, as he's offered to drive me back to Boynton.

There's a sense of disorientation inside the detective's car, and at first I think it must be from the shock of what I've experienced in the past three days . . . but then, it becomes clear that my surroundings are unfamiliar because this isn't my neighborhood; instead, it's an industrial part of the Bronx that I don't recognize. "Where are we?" I ask the detective as he's pulling his vehicle to the side of the street. Instead of responding, he quickly pivots his body from the driver's seat to move on top of me. My fingers fumble for the door handle that I can't locate until all I can grip is the armrest. I keep my eyes on a slice of light from an orange streetlamp overhead that's hitting the rearview mirror as his breaths are heavy and passionate in my ear.

In the span of a single week, three different men have taken what little sense of self I had—one of them a man who leads a congregation in faith of God's goodness, and another who swore an oath to serve and protect all citizens of this city. Two times now, I've seen that asking for help is a declaration that I'm alone and vulnerable, and it's an invitation for more danger. There will be no more trusting, no more fighting back—not only because I'm exhausted of all my strength, but because by now, at age sixteen, I understand:

I'm nothing more than a body to be abused.

3

TWO BIRDS IN A CAGE

There is rarely such thing as true recovery for the girl or woman who's been raped. There likely will never come a time in her life when the memory of what happened loses its sense of dark surreality, when she doesn't ask herself who she'd be if she'd never been left alone with that unfortunate person, in that unfortunate moment. Rape *is*. Once it happens to an individual, the experience now lives and breathes inside them, always. Rape is its own narrative, becoming part of the victim, taking away who she was before. This is something she always must carry.

This series of rapes and what they've revealed to me—that there are some people, even seemingly good people, who will hurt you—instills in me a pain and shame that makes it impossible to function for the first few days to follow. I return to the apartment of the well-intentioned neighbor who urged me to talk to the police. Out of her kindness and discretion, she asks nothing about how it went with the detective or what happened at the hospital. She assumes that my silence is connected to whatever happened to me *before* we went to the police.

I retreat quietly for a few days, staying inside her bedroom until her parents leave for work in the mornings, when I slip out and use the bathroom. Then I return to her bedroom and lie there, the occasional spell of sleep the only break from the memories of what's happened over the past week looping over... and over... and over in my mind. I ache to see Adrienne, and yet I cannot move. There is no such thing as someone I can trust. Now, everything I thought I knew about the people who are supposed to protect us is gone.

After several days, my friend tells me that her mother thinks it would be a good idea for me to go home.

The seven-year-old in me inquires innocently again: *Home? What is home?*

While I'm still living in the confusion of what has just happened, there is one thing that's clear: I can't be alone anymore. I have someone in this world, and that's my daughter. She's only two—she can't protect me, but she's the only person who loves me, who needs me, and whose life would be affected if something happened to me. Adrienne and I need each other.

I know that I have to be closer to Adrienne, but to live in the home of my adoptive parents again is not an option. Even if they would be willing to take me in, without a lock on my old bedroom door, I will never sleep in that apartment another night in my life.

The only possible solution I can work out is to find Theresa, a girl who lives in our building in Boynton who was one of the very few children I met when Roy and Daphne first brought me from Jamaica. Theresa is a couple years older than I am, but has always seemed young for her age. Daphne once stated that Theresa was not very "sharp," and maybe it was a certain lack of awareness about what might have been going on inside our home that made my adoptive parents deem her safe for me to befriend. I've always found her soft-spoken and sweet, a true friend to me.

When I ask around the building, I learn that Theresa is living in the apartment of her best friend, a girl named Rita, whom I met through Theresa when we were younger. Where Theresa's disposition is easygoing and maybe even a little naïve, Rita has always seemed a little harsher—more advanced, street smart. When I visit Rita's apartment, her mother says I'm welcome to stay awhile. "Is she sure?" I ask Rita, who assures me her mother loves having people in the apartment—she's Southern, after all. She and Theresa make space for my things inside Rita's bedroom, which we three will share.

Their late-night girl talk makes me feel like a part of something I've never experienced before. They both like fashion and share their wardrobes, encouraging and accessorizing me as I try on Rita's formfitting dresses and Theresa's more retro-inspired outfits. Early that fall, the two of them help me prepare for an interview I've gotten through the temp agency that finds work for them both. I get a job at Macy's as a clerical assistant with the head furniture buyer, taking the subway with the rush hour crowd into the city. Each morning before I leave, I run upstairs to the fourth floor to kiss Adrienne, who's always smiling with a full belly at breakfast time.

Because of the time I spent as a little girl in flea markets and thrift shops with Roy, I have an eye for good quality and an aptitude for the language in the furniture business. The assistant furniture buyer takes note of my interest in the work and suggests that I'd be a strong candidate for the store's assistant buyer program, where I'd learn about retail merchandising to prepare for an aptitude test in hopes to get on the company's executive track.

For an eighteen-year-old single mother with her GED, I know this is a big opportunity. I begin to invest myself more in work, traveling to the warehouse in Queens to learn about product from the two assistant buyers and signing up to play a small role in the store's planning for the Macy's Thanksgiving Day Parade.

For the first time in my life, I have girlfriends, a paycheck, and a feeling that I fit in. But just as my life is getting in order, it will take one relationship—followed by another—that will begin to take me drastically off track.

On Saturday nights, Rita, Theresa, and I go out dancing at night clubs around the city. This is when I meet Billy, a nineteen-year-old rapper in a group that's rocketing to fame with a new record and a video on MTV. Billy is confident, flirtatious, and he wins me over, asking me to marry him within a few months of meeting. We wed quickly and I take Adrienne out of Roy and Daphne's home and move both of us into his apartment in Harlem. Billy's mom watches Adrienne each day while I go to work and Billy's group tours the US. I find my daughter and myself with a man in our lives, as well as a home, and in-laws. For the first time, I'm surrounded with family. I place our marriage at the center of my life, putting on fresh bedding and doing Billy's laundry when he comes home from touring. We have meals and a schedule and a system to our life together when he's not out on the road or in the studio.

But when Billy returns from a tour in Canada, he rocks this long-awaited sense of stability when he requests that we bring another woman into our bedroom. *NO!* my heart screams out. Our love is sacred . . . but I agree, so used to dismissing my instincts and wanting to please him.

In the midst of all this, I learn that I'm pregnant again. "But I'm about to go on tour!" Billy pleads. "You really think this is a good time for us to have a baby?" When I share the news with his mother, she makes it clear that she's already got enough responsibility on her hands watching Adrienne while I work. "You just turned nineteen, Donna," she says. "Do you really want to have another baby?"

"I don't know what to do," I tell her.

"I do," she says. "I'll call the clinic to make the appointment if you're afraid." When I ask Billy what he thinks, his feelings are clear. The two of them talk me into terminating the pregnancy.

"This won't take long," the nurse tells me as she places a mask over my mouth and nose.

But I don't believe in abortions. I don't mind what other women do with their bodies, but I don't want to go through with this.

"No," I tell the nurse, blinking softly with wooziness. "I don't want to do this."

But the doctor moves in to stand over me. "It's already done," he tells me.

Instantly, my body begins to react to the news with the same shock as my emotions do. I shake with fever and begin to vomit, and the staff grows concerned because I'm bleeding so heavily that I've lost the color in my face. Everything about this decision was wrong. I can never, ever give this child his life back.

Weeks later, as I'm dealing with an infection from complications during the procedure, Billy comes to me and delivers the worst blow of all: he asks me for a divorce.

On top of the loss, the grief, the disappointment in myself, I feel stupid for having let my heart hope for more.

You are nothing, I remember. *Nobody will ever love you.*

Even the hurt of the divorce doesn't unravel my life as much as the abortion does. I cannot take another life…but after I do, I cannot live with myself for having done so.

In the second half of 1984 as I'm approaching my twentieth birthday, I enter a period of the worst self-judgment that I've ever felt in my life. My body is no longer carrying the miracle that was my baby. Instead, my psyche is carrying the combined weight of guilt, shame, sadness, grief. In my heart, I've always been able to hold on to that little piece of light—the hope that God was holding a space in my future for safety, and love. For happiness. But now, after my second child is gone, everything that anyone has ever told me about why they were abusing me is really true to me: I'm nothing. I've deserved all of this.

The moment that the pregnancy's been terminated, a spiritual warfare begins inside of me. I've committed an act against God. Not even He will love me anymore. I am still that alien, that lost little girl unworthy of any other person's love...and now unworthy even of God's love.

Emotionally, mentally, I spin and spiral down. I can't sleep, but I can't get myself out of bed. I stop showing up to work at Macy's, and soon, my manager calls Rita's house to inform me that I no longer have the job.

Finally Rita and Theresa step in with support to help me apply for another position through the temp agency. "It might do you some good to get out," they say. Just as the holiday season is about to begin, the agency places me in the 7 a.m. to 3 p.m. shift at a gift shop in the lobby of the Milford Plaza hotel in Times Square. With holiday decorations lighting up this section of the city and shoppers and visitors filling the streets, I find that this atmosphere lifts my spirits slightly from my grieving. The assistant manager at my new job, Dalida, is also incredibly kind. We bond quickly, and, craving as much connection in my life as I can get, I quickly begin to regard her like a sister.

During a quiet afternoon as we page through a fashion magazine together from the shop's newsstand, admiring images of Beverly Johnson, Dalida tells me that she's been doing some modeling on the side. *Modeling*, I think. *Yeah, that's what I want to do.* Maybe modeling could give me something positive to get excited about. If I were a model, I would actually *feel* beautiful without people having access enough to touch me or take advantage of me. Dalida says that after you have a good portfolio of photos, you can get booked for jobs that pay thousands of dollars. If this is true, then I could finally provide Adrienne with a really good life.

Dalida brings her portfolio to work to show me how she's started to book a few jobs. She explains that the key to booking work is to find a good photographer. Not wanting to bother her with all my questions, I begin to do some research on my own to try to find a photographer whose work I might be able to afford.

In January 1985, after Times Square has quieted down following the holidays, Dalida asks me whether I'd be willing to change my shift and work 3 p.m. to 11 p.m. It would make it easier for me to spend time with Adrienne in the day, but there's one aspect of the shift change that I'm not as enthusiastic about. "I won't get to see you anymore," I tell Dalida.

"Girl, when have you ever seen me go home on time?" she asks me. "You know I always stay late. You'll still see me almost every day."

I begin the night shift with another girl, named Maria, who's just recently been hired. With zero makeup and a wardrobe that reminds me of a librarian, Maria seems inhibited, unassuming, and dowdy. "Why are you talking to her?" Dalida whispers to me late one afternoon when she's working past the end of her shift.

"Because I *work* with her," I whisper back.

"Just be careful," Dalida says. "There's something about her I don't like."

"What do you mean?"

"I mean she's creepy. Something about her doesn't add up."

I know Dalida is smart, but seeing Maria as an outcast makes me want to befriend her even more. I know how it feels to be the person whom people treat differently.

When it's just Maria and me working at the store, I learn that she's three years older than I am. Her mother is from the Philippines, while her father, from Italy, owns a very successful business in Southeast Asia. Her father sounds powerful—he's friends with several world leaders, Maria says, and she shows me a letter that the pope personally wrote to her family. She also shares photographs from fancy family vacations, like when she toured the pyramids in Egypt. I'm awestruck by all of it, and curious to know more. "Whatever brought you to New York?" I ask her.

In response, Maria opens up to share some of her struggles with me. She's an only child and her father is very traditional Italian, so she feels that she has to prove herself just because she's a girl. "That's why I came to New York," she says. "To show him I can make it here." But she's having some trouble in her personal life—Maria is married and has twin toddlers, but her husband wants a divorce.

As conversations between young women go, all this prompts me to reveal to her some of my story. I tell Maria about the difficulties I've been facing, like my own separation. She knows about my daughter, who will turn four in February. I confide in her how hard life was with Alvin, and how I'm working hard to make a better life for Adrienne, who lives with my adoptive parents—another complicated relationship. I open up about some of the things I experienced inside Roy and Daphne's home when I was younger, and the fact that I ran away to Philadelphia and had to take a job parking cars to try to survive. "So you know how to drive?" she asks me.

"A little."

"Me too." There's an air of shared satisfaction between us, two young, independent women working to make it on our own in New York.

A couple times after our shift ends, the two of us go out for a bite to eat. Maria listens intently when I share background about my life with her. I can also relate to a lot of things she's experienced, including how difficult it is to please parents when they make you feel like you're never good enough, and how tough it is to create a sense of family in this city when you have roots in another country.

One night, Maria flips through bridal magazines from our gift shop's newsstand. "Why are you looking at those?" I ask her. She tells me that she's recently met a rich Swiss banker, and he's asked her to marry him. *A Swiss banker?! Her whole life is like a fairy tale,* I think. *If I hang out with her, maybe that could be me one day.* "I'll help you plan your wedding!" I tell her. We browse the magazines, and I tell her my dream is to be a model. "But Dalida says you have to pay a good photographer to take your pictures," I tell her.

"You need pictures?" says Maria. "I think I can help you."

"You can?"

"Sure," she says. "My godfather can help."

Then for the next few weeks, Maria and I don't cross paths. "Your friend Maria called," Rita tells me one night at home.

"She called here?" I scan my memory. *Did I ever give her my phone number?* "What did she say?"

"She left her phone number."

"Rita said you called!" I tell Maria the next day. "I was wondering where you've been."

"I've been to London to see the queen!" she says. "I'll tell you all about it—let's meet at the Sherry-Netherland hotel on Fifth Avenue," she says. "Then we'll go out from there."

The Sherry-Netherland sits at 59th Street, just diagonal from the Plaza Hotel and Central Park. From the entrance, I gawk inside at the lobby with its ornate crown molding and fresco on the ceiling. Under the black awning with a fancy gold clock, doormen help guests out of their taxis and limousines. I try to stay out of the way in the swirl of sights and activity as I wait for Maria while a gorgeous woman climbs into a car in front of me. I stand stunned for a moment: *That's Diana Ross!*

Just then, another dolled-up woman approaches me. She's wearing jeans and high heels, a short fur jacket, and makeup. I stare at her, confused. She starts laughing, and that's when I recognize her: it's Maria. "I've been standing here, watching you look for me all this time."

"Oh my God," I tell her. "Look at you!" She's so dressed up and glamorous that I didn't recognize her. She's a completely different person than the version of the Maria I know from work.

"Come on," she says. "Let's go get something to eat."

When we're seated inside a diner, she begins to tell me about her time away. "I saw my father," she says. "And guess what he told me?"

"What's that?"

"He told me he's *proud* of me."

"That's what you've wanted, isn't it?"

"Yeah. Now I have to really prove myself. What about you— what have you been up to?"

"Last week, I went to the Wilhelmina modeling agency."

"How'd that go?"

"They said they like my look, now I just have to come up with the money to pay a photographer."

"How much do you need?"

"Fifteen hundred dollars."

"That's easy," she says. "We'll call my godfather. Next week, come see me at my place in Queens. We can talk about how he can help you."

The following week, we meet briefly at a donut shop in Queens, where from her interactions with the staff, it's clear Maria is a regular. After we pay, we walk to her building where she lets me into an apartment—a small studio, much more than I'd ever be able to afford on my own. The living room is set up with a little table for dining right off of the kitchenette, and there's an area that's partitioned off with a curtain, presumably to be a bedroom. I try to calculate the details of Maria's life—her temp job, her marriage, her wealthy father—to determine how she's able to pay for her own place. "So," she says, interrupting my thoughts as she takes a seat at the kitchen table. "Tell me more about the modeling."

"Well," I say, joining her there, "I have to get a really good portfolio done. The thing is, that will cost more money than I've ever even seen."

"Let's call my godfather now," she says, reaching for the phone and dialing a number. "He's going to help you—don't worry about it." When a voice answers on the other line, Maria makes small talk for a moment before she shifts into the conversation about me. "I've got this friend," she tells the person on the line, and she relays everything I've just told her. "Sure," she says, then holds out the phone. "My godfather wants to talk to you."

I push through my shyness to move from the sofa and take the phone. "Hello?"

"Maria tells me a lot about you," I hear, with a brash New York accent, a conviction in this man's voice. "You treated her real nice at work, it sounds like. She likes you. Now. Tell me about this modeling."

Maria stands like a brick wall in front of me, her arms folded expectantly. My face grows hot under her stare as she observes my side of the conversation closely. "Yes," I tell him. "Modeling is my dream, but the problem is, I need fifteen hundred dollars. I've been thinking about getting another job—"

"Don't worry," the man says. "Anybody who's nice to Maria is a friend of mine. I'm gonna help you out."

"You are?" An excitement spikes inside of me. Maria takes

back the phone, and the two of them arrange for all of us to meet up. "It's a done deal," she says as she puts the phone in the cradle. "Next week. We'll all meet at the Milford Plaza."

"This is my godfather," she tells me a few days later in the hotel's lobby. "His name's Louis Miranda."

"But you don't need to call me that," he says. *Then what should I call you?* He's a little man, but grandiose in his speech and gestures in a way that urges me to keep my questions to myself.

I make eye contact with a tall Asian man who stands at Mr. Miranda's side, but it's as though Maria and Miranda pretend he's not there. As we four exit the hotel to walk to a nearby diner, Mr. Miranda engages in what appears to be an intense conversation with Maria while the Asian man utters not a single word. Once we're seated, Mr. Miranda launches into a series of stories using phrases like *the old times, the good times*, and names of people Maria appears to know. Then I hear a phrase that strikes me a little oddly: *la cosa nostra.*

Did I hear that clearly?

This is New York City in the mid-1980s, and there are stories in the news every day about mob-related killings. "Just look at Castellano!" Miranda says. The dealings of mob bosses like Paul Castellano, who is associated with the Gambinos and the Gotti family, appear in the headlines more and more. "Case in point. You see? Things get messy when you start to think you're bigger than the family."

What is he talking about? I must look perplexed, because Maria turns to me. "Just let him go," she laughs. "He just likes to talk."

"Anyways," says Miranda, calming to turn his attention to me. "So you want to model? Don't worry. I got people. I'll help you. Here's what we're gonna do: Maria, I want you to get everybody back together in a few days."

She already has the place picked out, she assures him, and a few days later, in March 1985, we gather again at the donut shop near her apartment. "I'm going to help you with this modeling thing," Miranda promises again inside the donut shop. "But I want you to do something for me."

"What's that?"

"Well, I have this partner, see. He wants to take me for my money, but that's not gonna happen, see. I'm going to get my money back, and here's what you're gonna do for me—" I look at Maria, whose eyes are fixed directly on Miranda. He leans toward me, across the table. "I want you to say that you saw my partner in a sexual thing with Maria."

I look at Maria. *Are you OK with this?* I want to ask her. But now, she's sitting back in her chair with a look on her face that's unfazed...even amused.

"He wants to play with me?" Miranda says. "Then I'm going to let his wife know the kind of guy he is. We don't play like that in the family!" he says, shaking his forefinger at me.

I listen, unsure of where this is going. "OK..."

"So next Wednesday night, he's gonna go on a date with my goddaughter"—he looks toward Maria—"and I want you to walk in. Then *you're* going to say you walked in, and you caught them fooling around, see—that's it!" I realize I must look confused when he says, "You don't understand what I said? That's all I want you to do. Do you think you could do that?"

I say nothing. Pressure is building in the pit of my stomach, but the more doubtful I feel, the harder he pushes me to agree.

"As a matter of fact," he says, "that's our deal. If you'll do that for me, *then* I'll give you the money you need for your modeling. Alright? That motherfucker. He thinks he's gonna take my money? Nuh-unh. Nope. We don't do like that in the family. OK?!" He yells this, as if I'm the one who's crossed him. *"Do you understand me?"*

"OK," I tell him. Daphne's instruction lives inside me: *An intelligent girl doesn't ask others questions, Donna Patricia.*

But, just like the questions in my childhood about how I could escape from Roy, this is a problem whose solution I won't find in the pages of any book…

And this is where it all goes wrong.

Miranda sets Wednesday, March 20 for Maria's date with his partner to take place. A few days before this, she calls me. "I need to see you one more time," she says.

Nerves rattle my insides as I travel from Boynton to Queens, where, again, I find Maria at the donut shop near her building. "Are we good?" she says as I take my seat. "You're my friend—are you still going to do it? If I do this for my godfather, my father will be very proud. I'm going to be looked at like a son. He's going to accept me."

"OK," I tell her. I care about Maria, and I know what it's like to crave the love and acceptance of a parent. "I'll do it." I replay my role as we've discussed it: all I have to do is walk in and see her on a date with Miranda's business partner.

"But we need more than one witness," she says. "It can't just be you walking in."

Again, not understanding this, I shrug. "OK."

"Who else do we know that could be a witness?" I stare at her, clueless as to what the role of this witness will even be. "It doesn't matter," she says. "I'll take care of it."

"Maria called tonight," Rita tells me as I hang my coat inside her closet.

"She did? But I just left her. Did she leave a message?"

"No," Rita says. "She wanted to talk to me. She asked if Theresa and I want to make some money."

"She did? What'd you say?"

"I told her yeah. Theresa too." Theresa recently had an ectopic pregnancy, and she's been struggling with medical bills ever since.

On Wednesday, March 20, my two roommates and I take the train from Boynton to Queens. First, this evening, we meet Miranda at the donut shop near Maria's apartment. Again, there's somebody with him—but it's not the Asian man who accompanied him to the Milford Plaza. Tonight his companion is an enormous black man with scars on his face and rotting teeth. "I arranged for somebody to go with you," Miranda tells us. "This is Woody. I want to make sure that nothing happens, and that the Bird knows that you witnessed him being with Maria in this encounter."

The Bird? I look at Woody, who stays quiet. There's something about him that's animalistic…not human. Miranda pulls out a set of keys from his pocket and hands them to Woody. "Come on," Woody says. His voice is deep and demonic. "It's time to go to the apartment."

Exiting the diner are Theresa, Rita, Woody, and me. When we reach Maria's apartment building, Woody turns and passes me the keys. He stares at me until I accept the key ring and open the door to Maria's apartment. Then I walk in, stepping to the side so that Rita, Theresa, and Woody can also come in. I watch as Woody closes the door behind us. Then he puts out his hand as a clear instruction for me to return the keys to him, which I do.

When we're inside the apartment, we face Maria's combined living and dining space. Suddenly, a small Asian man appears in the kitchenette, a different man than the one who we met at the Milford Plaza. *Where did he come from?* Then Maria also appears—she must have been hiding somewhere. *Why are they all here?*

Woody and Maria start whispering with the Asian guy, while I look at Rita and Theresa. *Something's off,* our gazes agree, and then we all spot movement on the sofa—a man lies on his side, with his back facing us. He's stirring slightly, and when I get a good look, he's handcuffed. Wearing nothing but a white, button-down shirt, a pair of boxers, and dark socks, he moans quietly.

My senses are heightened in alarm. Rita, Theresa, and I hold each other's eyes, all three of us panicked and confused. We haven't walked in to find an intimate scene, like Miranda and Maria told us to anticipate.

Woody turns toward us from the huddle of conversation with Maria and the Asian man. "Sit down," he says to Theresa, Rita, and me. In quiet uncertainty, the three of us squeeze onto the love seat, Rita and Theresa on either side of me. We watch as the Asian guy exits, sliding out of Maria's apartment door and closing it quietly behind him.

Maria turns to Woody. "Did my godfather give you the thing?" she says. "Did he get it fixed?"

"Yeah."

"Let me have it." Woody reaches inside his jacket and pulls out a brown paper bag, which he hands to Maria. She opens it, looks inside...and then her face breaks into a smile. Slowly, she pulls out the contents of the bag: it's a nickel-plated pearl-handle revolver.

My mind stops. My heart stops. *Maria has a gun in her hand.*

Rita and Theresa are likewise still, both looking on in fear. There's not a breath of motion among us three.

"Plans have changed," Woody announces. "This is what Boss Man wants." His voice booms with depth as he continues...but as I stare into the black hole of the revolver, I don't hear a word Woody says. All I can hear are Dalida's words:

I told you not to trust her!

Maria aims the gun at my face. "Donna," she says, "we know where you live."

No.

"And we know about your daughter. What Woody said is right: my godfather changed plans. This is what's going to happen..."

I stare up at her, knowing my face can't hide my fear.

"You need to understand that if you don't do exactly as we say, we're going to kill your daughter—in fact, we'll kill your whole family."

Because I've shared stories about my upbringing with Maria, she knows this threat will complicate my mind. I imagine Adrienne's brown eyes, wide in uncertainty as Roy and Daphne—both tormented, scared, suffering—try to shield her from violence. No matter what happened to me inside their home, I don't want them to be hurt.

Maria turns the gun's aim from me toward Rita, then to Theresa. *If she keeps moving it around like that, one of us will end up shot!* "We know you both have families, too," she says. "Donna, you're going to get the car. Woody's going with you."

"You're driving," Woody tells me. I feel sweat break across my forehead. Like a hurricane tide crashing onto the shore, a sudden awareness comes rushing at me: Maria kept score of every detail of every story that I've shared about myself with her. Right now, there is no weighing of risks—when my eyes fell on the shiny end of her gun and she mentioned my daughter, I understood that the scale was tipped completely against me. I can't try to escape, and I can't pretend that I don't know how to drive. She remembers my telling her that I parked cars in a garage when Alvin took me to Philadelphia. She used that information to plot this with Woody and Miranda, and who knows who else.

I paid close attention to everything she revealed to me, too… but I'm so naïve! Instead of questioning her overconfidence as she told me her extravagant stories, I looked up to her. There were so many signs that something wasn't right: the way her appearance had transformed outside the Sherry-Netherland hotel, the story about the Swiss banker who proposed to her, even though she's still legally married. *Did* she meet the queen of England? I believed that Maria was going to show me the way to an easier life. Meanwhile, the whole time I'd been admiring her, she'd been sitting back, watching me, angling how she could use my trust to get what she wants: her father's praise.

I have to walk quickly to keep up with Woody's Goliath steps, until we locate a white Cadillac with a burgundy roof. "Get in," he says, again handing me keys. I take the driver's seat, knowing I have no choice but to do what they say until I can manage some way out of this. If I go to Roy and Daphne, they'll only dismiss me, chase me out, and probably accuse me of making this up. If I go to the police—

No. I can't go to the police alone ever again.

"Drive back around to the apartment," Woody says. I've never driven a car in the city, and I'm not experienced to navigate the one-way streets in this neighborhood in Queens. I work to appear as though I'm keeping my cool as he watches my hands closely. "Park here," he says when we've reached Maria's building. "Stay in the car. Keep the lights off." Dusk sets in early on these first evenings of spring, but I sit quietly with all the car lights shut off. I know that any deviation I make from the instructions Woody's given me could be the difference between life and death. I watch as the hulk of his figure reenters Maria's building. He moves like the black version of Jaws from the James Bond movies: big, calculated, demented. My mind throbs with fear for Rita and Theresa. What are they about to experience inside? The only thing I can be sure of about Maria is that I can't be sure of anything.

Through the apartment doors, Woody and Theresa come fumbling out of the building on either side of the staggering man, whose dress slacks I can see under the trench coat they've draped over his head. *Oh…my God.* Maria opens the back door of the car. "If anybody asks, he's drunk," she says, shoving him into the backseat.

"Don't let him sit up," Woody says. He and Maria maneuver the man so that he's sitting on the backseat floor of his own car. Rita and Theresa slide into the car, followed by Woody and Maria. By the time we all pile in, six adults are packed into this Cadillac. "Go to Harlem," Woody says.

I turn the key in the ignition. "Alright but…I don't know the way there."

Woody directs me toward I-278, across Randall's Island and onto the FDR parkway, where he tells me to take the northbound ramp. Once we're in Harlem, he tells me the way to a redbrick apartment building on the corner of 143rd Street and Seventh Avenue. "Stop the car," Maria says. "Wait here." It's clear she's the captain of this operation, having taken orders as direct communication from Miranda. Together, she and Woody wrangle the man's body, still limp and lumbering, out of the backseat and begin to drag him upstairs.

I stay in the car, still dumbstruck by all this, except for one thing: something's not right. What's happening is very different from walking in and witnessing an intimate scene between a man and a woman. I don't know what to expect, what any of this means...or what lies ahead.

It feels like years have passed in the course of a few hours as it nears midnight, when Woody and Maria send Rita, Theresa, and me to park the man's Cadillac at a garage in the Bronx—specifically, where it will be out of sight but close to a bridge, Maria says. "You'll take the train back here in the morning," Maria says to us girls. "We'll call you early—and if you don't answer, remember: we're coming for you." If we do anything out of line, she says, or if she and Woody get the impression that we have any intentions to tell anyone about this, they will do exactly what they said they would do to our families. To my daughter. "And don't even think about going to the police," Maria says. "My godfather has friends in the police."

Remembering my own experience with the police, I don't breathe a word to Rita and Theresa about the possibility of contacting them. On the drive back to the Bronx, I say nothing at all—the three of us are silent with overwhelm, exhaustion...fear. For the first time, I feel separate from my two closest friends. We three occupy this car together, but there's a sense that we're all alone. We can't save each other from this: not Theresa with her sweetness, not Rita with her wits, not me with my insistence to try to see the goodness in everyone. There is no bright side to any of this.

Yet again, I trusted someone when I shouldn't have. I thought Maria was lonely, different, that she just needed a friend who would give her a chance. But now I understand all that was a setup. Maria has two sides, and one is a completely different person than the innocent co-worker I thought I knew. *This is all your fault, Donna.* And this is what I get. Over and over, people in my life disappoint me. I don't know why I can't stop searching for someone I can believe in.

That night, back at Rita's apartment, there is no sleep. I can feel the other two lying awake, but the only movement happens when Rita jumps up and races to the kitchen when the phone rings before the sun has come up. "They want us to go," she says when she returns to the bedroom, strung out with grogginess. Before 6 a.m., we're on the train back to Harlem.

As Maria instructed Rita, we enter an apartment building on 143rd Street, all of us walking lightly up the stairs until a door opens a slight crack and we find ourselves in the entry of what must be someone's home...a term one can only use lightly. As we three inch down the hallway toward a main room, I have to subtly shield my nose to avoid getting sick from the thick smells of mildew and body odor. Early morning light tries to break through the windows and a couple of lamps are turned on, but it's dark and dirty here in every sense. Inconspicuously, I go into survival mode and try to take in my surroundings. *There's the bathroom. There's the kitchen*—but it doesn't look like any place I'd want to eat in. This is the living area, where we're standing. It's bare, just like Roy and Daphne's home was. I spot one bedroom, then a second bedroom; and that's where I spot him: the man they refer to as the Bird is spread-eagle, bound to the full-sized bed with a gag in his mouth and a blindfold over his eyes. One of his wrists is fastened with handcuffs to a spindle of the wooden headboard, while the other wrist is bound with a cloth. His ankles are fixed to the footboard with the same type of cloth, and though his mouth is gagged, every now and again he tries to muster enough energy to try to say something. Unlike the rest of the apartment, there's an overhead light lit. This room is the brightest space in the apartment, but from this, the main room, I can see that the curtains have been closed so that not a splinter of light can come through.

When I bring my attention back to my immediate surroundings, perched across from us is a woman whose figure weighs down her cot, which is constructed of milk crates supporting a yellow padded foam mattress. In all of my life, I've never seen anyone of such colossal size.

With a small TV set up next her, it appears this living area has been made into a makeshift bedroom to accommodate her size. My senses take in her features at turbo-speed: her lips collapsed around bare gums; her short, spiky braids; the hairs that stick out from her chin. She reminds me of one of the Obeah witches my mother might have worshiped with in Jamaica.

Placed around the room are three plain wooden chairs, bare minimum, like everything in this apartment...including the cleaning job. "What's your name, sweetie? Sweetie!" she hollers. Rita and Theresa nudge me to speak. "I'm Selma, and I want to know, what is your name?"

It takes everything inside of me not to turn and run…but then Maria and Woody emerge. "Sit down," Woody says. Maria moves in beside him.

Seeing no option but to comply, Rita, Theresa, and I take seats in the empty wood chairs. Maria steps up in front of us—now with the gun again. "My godfather's on his way," she says. "He'll tell you the plan."

Rita, Theresa, and I sit in petrified silence.

Minutes later when Miranda walks in, he keeps his eye on us three girls as he speaks quietly with Maria and Woody. "This is what you do," he finally says to Rita, Theresa, and me. "Maria's going to get a rental car, and you—" he looks at me—"you're going to drive it. You two," he says to Rita and Theresa, "you're going to stay here and help take care of him. You do whatever these three tell you, you understand?" Woody stands over us in a way so menacing that I turn my face down, waiting for him to hit me.

"Just so it's clear," Miranda says, "this is not a joke. And this motherfucker in there, he owes me money. I'm going to get my money, see. That's all I care about." He turns to Maria. "Did you tell them what would happen?"

"I told them," she says.

"I'm gonna tell them again." Miranda goes on to repeat what Woody and Maria have already stated: if we don't do anything that they tell us to do, they'll kill my daughter. Then he turns to Rita and Theresa. "And trust me, we know all about your families, too." He mentions Rita's mother, referring to her by her first name. It's obvious they've done some research about each of our families.

From this moment, I am numb, in autopilot just to try to make it through. For the next ten days, Rita and Theresa don't leave the apartment.

I stay there with them almost constantly, but because I can drive, I leave only when I'm directed to pick up Miranda at a building he owns in midtown Manhattan. I transport him all over the city to various destinations at all hours of the day and night, sometimes with Maria or Woody accompanying him. In these cases, they tell me where to drive, always to buildings on Long Island, Staten Island, Queens, and Manhattan, often in Chinatown or a building that Miranda owns on the east side of midtown, very close to where Paul Castellano will later be murdered. On occasion, Maria takes the wheel as Miranda directs me to the passenger seat while he goes in the back. I sit in silence when they climb out of the car to tour buildings in all these different locations. When they return, I hear phrases like *doing business with the Chinese* and *We have to make it look like the Asians did this.* I do what I can to tune my mind out. I don't want to know anything more about them or what they do, but I can't help but pick up on the fact that Woody and the big woman, Selma, seem to be a couple who have worked for Miranda for years. They're accustomed to going after people to settle bad deals on behalf of "the Boss Man."

This continues for more than a week. Not a single minute passes when I don't ask myself if Adrienne is alright with Roy and Daphne. Every time I return to the apartment, I can see that Rita and Theresa are unraveling—drained, numb, exhausted like me. "Are you OK?" one will ask the other on occasion. We nod curtly to each other in response, not wanting to discuss what each of us is experiencing or witnessing.

One day when I go to pick up Miranda at one of his buildings in midtown, he tells me: "Go into the bedroom." I enter as he instructs me, believing that maybe he needs me to get something for him—but at once he closes the door and charges at me. He puts his hand on my throat and shoves me onto the bed, where it takes me a few seconds to realize what's happening before I can begin to fight back. He braces one arm over my neck and props himself up with the other arm. I contest him, but ultimately, he gets what he wants.

This act of rape becomes yet another prison for my soul, just like what happened with Alvin, with the detective . . . and just like what happened when I became a Hylton. But with Miranda, with all the other circumstances happening and his business partner who's fighting for his life, the abuse is more than just traumatic. There's no way that I can even figure out a healthy way of getting out of the situation. I notice that I don't feel ashamed. I'm disgusted—disgusted with myself because I don't know what to do.

When he's finished with me, Miranda says, "Let's go." Angry and repulsed—at him, at life, but most of all, at myself—I drive him back to Harlem, where for the first time, the victim is sitting up with the gag from his mouth removed. Woody's holding a knife to his throat and a tape recorder next to his mouth with a piece of paper on it. "You read exactly what's written here," Woody says through gritted teeth. "Do you understand me?"

Miranda walks in the bedroom ahead of me then approaches his business partner. He grabs the man by the back of his hair and then begins to slap him. "You thought you were going to take my money, you stupid son of a bitch?" he says. "Nobody takes my money!"

I stay outside the room, my stomach tight with emotion. I know what it feels like to be constrained, abused, trapped and held with no dignity, to be the one hurting, while others stand by. Maria lights a cigarette and takes a puff, then, when the ash glows orange with heat, she squeezes the butt of the cigarette between her fingers and carefully holds the hot tip to the man's leg. When he cries out in response, I can literally feel his pain. The smell of singed flesh takes me back to when Alvin used to do that very same thing to me. Every moment is an overload to my senses. "Read this!" Woody tells the man, the edge of the knife making a crease across the skin of the Bird's throat.

"Why are you doing this?" the man weeps.

Woody and Miranda react in violent agitation. "Read what's on the fucking paper!"

He blinks hard to focus his eyes and finds strength enough to read steadily. After they finally get the recording they want, they stick the tape inside a manila envelope. "You're coming with me," Maria tells me as she and Miranda see me out of the apartment. On the street, she gets into the driver's seat of Miranda's car. "Get in," she says. "You're going to drop that off."

"No," Miranda says, as if it's just occurred to him that they can't trust me. "Maria, you take it in. You," he says to me. He never calls me by name. "You go in with her." We drive through Queens toward Long Island, arriving at a small office building in a suburban area.

"Come on," says Maria.

"Hey!" Miranda calls. I stop from exiting the passenger side to turn to him. "Don't you say a *word* to these guys," he says. "Do you hear me?"

Slowly, I nod and exit the car. Inside the office, I stay quiet while Maria has a very brief conversation and hands off the envelope. This exchange will be a turning point in this whole saga, but I don't know that just yet.

When we return to the apartment later that morning, I ask Rita and Theresa: "Is he eating? Has anybody fed him?"

Sad, they both shake their heads: *No.*

"He has to eat," I say, my urgency quickly building. "He has to eat. He can't not eat!" I tell Maria: "This man has to eat!"

"I'm not going to feed him," she grunts.

Woody comes in. "Feed him? What the fuck are you talking about, 'feeding him'?"

I know my life is on the line, but I can't watch this for another second. This man hasn't eaten for at least two days. I have nothing to lose anymore, and I can't continue to witness this torture and suffering. "He has to eat," I say. "I said HE HAS TO EAT!"

"Who's going to feed him?" Woody grabs me and yanks me into the living room. "Are you going to be here to feed him?"

My emotion continues to rise; it's as if my own survival is dependent on his. "He has to eat—he can't be here without eating! We have to feed him!"

Maria grabs me. "She's losing it," she tells Woody. "Let's go."

Together we walk downstairs to the bodega that occupies the ground level of the apartment building. "Get him something," she tells me, out of the clerk's earshot. "Just nothing he has to chew."

I take off down the aisle. Maria stands back impatiently while I storm through the store, ultimately choosing cherry Kool-Aid and some soup broth in a can.

Back in Selma's dingy kitchen I find a pan to warm the broth and a plastic cup that I rinse out and try to scrub clean with hot water and my bare hands. Then I switch on the faucet to let the cold water run from the sink, pouring the Kool-Aid mix into the cup and stirring the pink powder so it dissolves bright red into the liquid.

Inside the bedroom, the man holds his head up weakly, not having eaten or drunk in days. I remove his gag, and as I place the cup to his lips to drink, I have to move away out of fear he might choke, as he gulps out of thirst. As we develop a rhythm to this exchange—me, serving small sips; him, swallowing with grateful relief—I alternate feeding him tastes of each to allow him some degree of the feeling that he's having an actual meal.

Angry, Woody tramps into the doorway. "Who's going to take him to the bathroom?" he says. As though I can't hear him, I continue to feed the man.

"Can I please have a cigarette?" he whispers to me. His head is tilted up toward me, but with the blindfold on, he's not entirely sure of where my face is in relation to his own. It strikes at my heart to realize that there is something so deeply disempowering about not being able to see what's happening around you. It would be easier to excuse myself and step away from the pain of witnessing his vulnerability in this moment—but I refuse to leave him by himself. "Please?" His voice cracks with physical weakness.

I turn to look at Maria, who's heard the exchange from where she's taken Woody's place in the doorway. "Go ahead," she says, disgusted with my concern for this man. I go to his raincoat, fumbling past the London Fog tag to find Pall Mall cigarettes inside the inner pocket. I put a cigarette to his mouth, and Maria gives me a lighter. "Just for a minute," she says. The flame catches on the cigarette and he sucks it with a hunger that is different, more needy than that for drink or food. Again, we establish a rhythm while I try to give him as much of the cigarette as Maria will allow. This moment is the first time in days that I have felt any sense of personal strength—that I can provide him with some comfort; some sense of kindness or humanity.

"What's your name?" he asks me. His skin is gray with unrest, his lips are dry and cracking, beginning to peel. His voice is raspy, quiet in his understanding that he needs to keep our interaction private.

I hesitate for a moment to respond, not only because he's putting us both in danger by chatting, but also because the thought of relating to him in conversation makes it all the more heartbreaking to see him bound and struggling for his life. Even if he did steal money from Miranda or anyone else, no one deserves to be treated like this for days that are now turning into more than a week. Face-to-face like this, I can't find it in myself to dismiss or ignore him. I pull the cup of Kool-Aid away from his mouth and brace it between my hands. "Why do you want to know my name?"

"Because," he says. "You're different. You're different than the others."

I stare at him, his head cocked awkwardly toward me, as though I could feed him compassion just the way I've been feeding him food. *You're different.*

You're different.

That word he uses to describe me—"different"—is exactly the way I've felt all my life. However, it's here, in the total gloom of this moment in the worst experience of my life, that I feel something for the first time in all my twenty years: he sees my being different in a way that's positive. In this unlikely moment when we're both at our weakest, we're able to forgive each other for the mistakes we both made to end up here. In his request for kindness, he's showing the same to me. This man has had a blindfold over his eyes every day since I've met him, but still, even he can see that there's goodness in my character. *He's right,* I think. *I'm not like them.*

And then my rational voice weighs in: *But if you're not like them, Donna, then how did you get here?*

I continue to feed him, pushing the negativity out of my mind to be present for this man and feeling the rare fullness of myself, a sense of empowerment, in this moment. I've always been the one begging for help and mercy, never the one in a position to challenge what was happening around me and extend that help. When he finishes with the Kool-Aid and broth, I call Rita and Theresa in to help me guide him into the bathroom. We give him privacy as he uses the toilet, and together, we three young women wash him up. I sprinkle Shower to Shower on him from the shelf, knowing that forever from this day, the soap-clean scent of it will transport me back to this rusty bathroom with mold climbing the walls. "You're different than the others," he repeats as I prepare to stand him up. "Will you help me?"

I pause from leading him out of the bathroom and think for a moment about how I could get us both out of here. Finally, all I can give him is the truth. "How can I help you?" I ask him. "I can't even help myself."

Can't you just get Miranda his money? I want to ask him as we walk back toward the bedroom. *Then maybe we could all go home.* I don't realize yet that it's not that simple, that by the time someone is being tortured for money, there's not a quick phone call or visit to the bank teller that will make it all go away. I can already sense that this experience has been a defining point in my life—no matter how this ends, there will never be any going back.

As he takes his place back on the bed, I begin to rewind the events beginning from the very first step into Maria's apartment. I'd agreed to witness a guy on a date with Maria. I *did not know* they were kidnapping him. When I said yes to this, I said yes as a young single mom, struggling for money and thinking some extra cash would help me start a life for my daughter and me to have a home together. I want to be present for her in the way my birth mother was not. I never imagined that one decision—one single agreement to enter a friend's apartment—would completely change my life.

But when Friday night arrives, April 5, 1985, it's been two weeks start to finish since this whole thing began. When Maria and I return to the apartment from a few errands she directed me to drive her on, we find Rita and Theresa sitting silently, spent, while Woody and Selma mouth off to each other over the volume of the TV. Seeking some way out, even just a few minutes alone, I take a Heineken beer that Woody has brought in. Their larger bedroom is lit only by a dull lamp when I enter and walk to the window. Outside, the city night seems extra dark. *Would you help me?* I hear him ask again. *You're different. You're not like the others.*

Help him, I tell myself. *Help him. Help him!*

I know what I can do: I can pray. I turn to the dresser, where I've noticed a Bible resting. I pick it up and sit on the edge of the bed, placing my beer on the nightstand.

But when I open the Bible, I don't find what I'm looking for. Instead of pages, there's the empty space of a hollow box. The only symbol of God in this entire place is fake. I lift its only contents— one tiny amber bottle with a cork top that I turn between my thumb and finger. I examine it, finding a white label that reads in black typed lettering: DEVIL'S ROOT.

I drop it back into the wooden Bible box and slam the top shut. I flash back, inside the stone cave, a little girl with chants and spells and burning herbs going up all around her. I look at the ceiling, wishing I could rise away from here the way I could back then. *You are not here,* I say to God. *Just like my mother and anyone I've ever needed to help me...you've abandoned me, too.*

I deserve this.

I wake up to the feeling of Maria shaking my leg while Rita stands next to her. Peeping through the window is the faintest gray of morning light. "What's wrong?"

Rita seems to look past me with vacant eyes. "He's not breathing," she says.

"What?"

"He's not breathing. He's not breathing!"

"He's not breathing." Maria's words are the same as Rita's, but with a smirk of satisfaction, her reaction is very different.

I rise from the bed and race toward the other bedroom with Rita following on my heels. We both stand behind the width of Selma, who's blocking the doorway. In two weeks, this is the first time I've seen her off of her makeshift cot.

"What's going on?" Woody says, now also gathering with all of us outside the bedroom.

"He's not breathing," Rita says, shaking her head in disbelief. "He's not breathing."

"No," I whisper. "No. No." I start screaming. "No! No! No!" I shove past Selma. "He's breathing!" I yell. "Look—he's breathing! He's breathing! Look! He's breathing! He's breathing! Look! LOOK!"

Woody busts through and slaps me. I hold my face and turn,

dazed, toward the living room, where I drop into a chair. *I know he's breathing. Nothing can convince me right now that he's not breathing.* My mind can't accept any other possibility than that he's still alive.

"We have to let Boss Man know," Woody announces, but I'm still too much in a mental fog to pay attention to what's going on—until I hear Woody's plan. "I'm going to get a trunk from my apartment, and find some rocks."

A trunk? Rocks?

This is not real.

"I just talked to Miranda," Maria says, now standing over me in the living room. This time, I refuse to look at her. "Did you hear me? I talked to Miranda. He says we have to take the rental car back and go to Queens to pick up a van."

I'm silent, overwhelmed, on the drive to Queens. We reach a rental garage, and Maria works with the clerk to rent a large white van. Woody returns just as we make it back to Selma's apartment. I take a seat, still in too much shock to pay attention to what's going on around me—but Maria says the car rental agency in Queens just called to inform her that there was a problem with her payment for the van. They tell her to go to their other garage, which is located in Manhattan.

Again, it's my job to accompany her and Woody to the car rental garage on 96th Street between West End and Tenth Avenue. Maria gets out to take care of the payment while I sit in the van with Woody. "Go in with her," Woody tells me.

I climb out of the van, but when my feet hit the concrete, I'm so catatonic with exhaustion—disoriented by what's just happened—that it seems the rental office grows farther from me with every step that I take to reach it. When I finally step inside the lobby, I hang back by the door as my mind is only present enough to take in the facts of my surroundings: Maria standing at the desk to the left, the male clerk behind the counter who's talking to her, two men in jeans filling out paperwork on clipboards in the waiting area. I watch as the two of them rise from their chairs to approach the clerk. "You're under arrest!"

Maria turns slowly as each of the men stand with guns pointing at her. Then one of them takes my hands, puts them behind my back, and cuffs me. In this moment, my subconscious makes a distinct calculation whose outcome will only point to a conclusion that I don't want to believe: if these are real police and they're arresting me, then I have to accept that the man has in fact died. With my mind skewed by the events, the only consideration I allow myself to make in a fraction of a second is that this is some test set up by Miranda.

But within minutes, policemen from the NYPD swarm the scene. As they pull me outside and escort me to the backseat of an unmarked car, I begin to allow the weight of the possibility to set in: maybe this *is* real.

Then they drive me beneath the rental office to an underground garage, where minutes later, more officers arrive with Maria and another group with Woody. The three of us are held separately, though I'm not in a state of mind where I care to see either of them.

My mind continues to wrestle with the death that now apparently has happened.

In the hours they hold me here, I learn more background about the crime than I'd known in the previous several weeks. Miranda and his business partner had been together on the selling side of a real estate transaction in which Miranda accused his partner—named Tom Vigliarolo, I learn—of swindling him out of figures that the police say ranged anywhere between $160,000 to nearly half a million dollars. Capturing his partner and holding him was Miranda's attempt to get the money back, while plotting and overseeing the whole operation was Maria's way of proving to her father, another close partner of Miranda, that she could be as tough and successful at their business schemes as the men in her family are.

The policemen in plainclothes were from the Nassau County Police Department on Long Island, where the victim's wife waited several days to report him as missing because he routinely spent days at a time away from home to work in the city. But when Maria delivered the tape recording to his office on Long Island and I accompanied her, the guys in the office remembered that Thomas had planned a date with Maria behind his wife's back, making Maria the last person to have seen him before he went missing. As they put the pieces together, they contacted his wife. That's when she called her local police.

"What do you know about this real estate business?" police from the NYPD ask me.

"I don't know anything, except what I heard them say in the car."

"Is he alive?" they ask me. "Is he alive?" *Yes*, I want to tell them, because it's what I want to believe. *Yes, he's alive. Can somebody tell me how he is?* "I don't know if he's alive," I tell them somberly. "I *want* him to be alive. But I don't know."

A few hours later when they circle me back to 143rd Street, there are helicopters hovering above the apartment building, bright lights high on poles to illuminate the scene, cameras, reporters buzzing around to collect information. The police leave me in the car while they go up in the apartment. I crane my neck to look out the window just as a lightning storm of camera flashes shine on the faces of two people I recognize: Rita and Selma. Theresa had a follow-up appointment with her OB/GYN in Boynton, which Miranda told her to keep so that no suspicion would be stirred by her absence at the doctor's office.

Before I witness any indication of whether the man is still alive, the police pull out. For the next thirty-six hours they drive me around the city—throughout Manhattan, out to Queens, and to Long Island. They take forensic samples: my fingerprints, hair from my head, and hair from my private parts. My stomach roars with hunger, but I don't dare ask to eat. The pain that's making me sicker than my hunger is wondering what's happening with my daughter now that I've been arrested. One of the police officers accuses me of having lied about not knowing whether the man was dead, but they don't understand what was going on: I didn't believe that he was dead. I had cared for that man. I *couldn't* believe it.

I'm interrogated by NYPD officers at the 32nd Precinct. Here, I stay several nights in a cell by myself, restless, but so spent that

I'm able to get small spells of sleep here and there. After a few days there, I face a small team of attorneys sitting across a conference table at the office of Robert Morgenthau, the district attorney of New York County. "My daughter's life was in danger," I tell them. "Before we start, can someone please make sure she's OK?"

"What do you mean your daughter's life was in danger?"

"They threatened to kill her if I didn't do what they said. Please—can someone check on her?"

"You use our time together this morning to tell us what you know," one of the lawyers says. "And we'll check on your daughter."

I volunteer the little information that I have. After hours of asking me the same questions in dozens of different ways, they ask me to sign a statement, which I do. If they'll check on Adrienne, I'll do anything to cooperate.

At close to midnight, the police officers take me in an NYPD cruiser on a drive almost an hour away. They start north in Manhattan, over the East River and into Queens, finally leaving an island of trees and greenery to enter onto a bridge. To my right, out the passenger-side window, I can see the runway of LaGuardia Airport—the place I landed when I first arrived in this country thirteen years ago. I watch the flashing lights of a plane take off, soaring into the sky above us, like a butterfly in the air. Since I arrived in this city, I've dreamed of the day I could make my own choices for my life. Now it may be possible that I'll never experience that freedom.

After a couple of minutes, toward the end of the bridge, a road sign reads SLOW DOWN—but it feels as though the van actually picks up speed as a high chain-link fence with barbed wire emerges. The bridge meets land again, in a forest of fences and concrete. This is Rikers Island.

It's late at night when they bring me into a receiving room. I still have not eaten, and I haven't slept more than a few short hours at a time for what's now three weeks.

One staff member stands under the curtain of an old tripod camera to take my photograph. "May I use the phone?" I ask the officer at the receiving room desk.

He looks up at the clock. "Who do you need to talk to at two a.m.?"

"I need to call home," I tell him. "To check on my daughter."

He refuses to look at me when he nods toward the phone. I dial Roy and Daphne's number and hold my breath as the line rings once...then twice. At the third ring, I prepare to hang up, somewhat relieved there's no answer—then suddenly, I hear Roy's voice, gravelly with sleep. "Yeah?" he says. I rest my forehead against the wall in front of me. *Nobody will ever love you the way I do.* The memory of my adoptive father's words ten years ago are a weight in my mind that have a way of pulling me down, down, always farther down, no matter how low I'm already feeling. *If you ever loved me, as your daughter or anything else,* I want to tell him, *then can you please help me right now?* "What is it?" he says impatiently.

"I just thought I should call."

He grumbles, clearly irritated. "Where are you calling us from?" His use of the word *us* strikes me, as though suddenly he and Daphne are one entity, as though my absence, my failure, has somehow unified them.

I think twice for a moment...but I have no choice but to answer his question. "I'm at Rikers Island."

From this point, he's purely matter-of-fact. He doesn't ask about the crime or how I am; he only tells me that the police have been to the apartment to question them. "They asked what we knew," he says. "But we didn't know anything. They showed up a second time—"

"To check on Adrienne?"

"No. The district attorney's office wanted us to tell them you're a bad mother."

"Did you tell them I love my child?"

"I didn't get involved," he says. Immediately, I know why: he'd be subject to questioning about my upbringing, and he doesn't want his own history to be exposed in the midst of all this.

"How is Adrienne?" I ask him. I feel the muscles in my face tense up uncontrollably as I try to keep my voice strong. "I'd do anything to see my little girl."

"Adrienne is fine," he says.

Will you bring her here to see me?!

"Here," he says. "I'll pass you to your mother."

I can picture Daphne taking the phone, caught off guard and slightly rumpled from sleep but still properly coiffed. I hold the telephone with both hands, ready to pull it from my ear if she screams. Instead, she has one calm, singular point to tell me: "I didn't put you in this situation." A rustle comes through the phone as she hands it back to Roy. Then the line goes dead.

How I'm faring isn't even a question in her mind.

The combination of loneliness, guilt, and shame—the desperation to be loved—threatens to put me over the edge. Since Mr. V died, I've been drowning in emotions; in disturbance and distress and unable to live with myself. Now these emotions begin to boil up inside me and give way to anger: *Why don't you care?* I want to scream at my adoptive mother. *Can't you just ask how I'm doing, this once? If you'd ever listened to me when I asked you for help, I wouldn't be here!* I didn't run away because I wanted to—I ran away because it was safer than staying in the home of a pedophile! Instead, the only help I found was Alvin—someone who beat out of me what was left of my self-worth.

As I dialed their number, I was foolish enough to hope that they might offer me some kind of legal help, or that they'd arrange to bring Adrienne to see me. When we hang up, I know: Roy and Daphne were my only prayer out of this. They brought me to this country and called me their daughter. They're the only ones I can turn to, and they won't even help me now, when I need a family more than ever.

"I just saw you in the news." I turn around to find a fellow inmate working behind the registration desk. I cast down my eyes. "Have you eaten?" she says.

Now I look up at her. I've lost track of days. I'm unsure when my last meal was. I take a moment to feel for my appetite, which seems to have disappeared when the phone went dead . . . but I will gratefully accept any kindness that's extended to me right now.

"We've got some food left from dinner, here—I'll go heat some up for you." When she returns carrying a tray of rice and a patty of chicken, I try to eat slowly, the way Daphne taught me when I was a child. I realize quickly, however, that my appetite is stronger than my manners. "They're working to find you a housing unit," this inmate tells me.

When I finish eating, she and an officer work together to register me and give me a pile of belongings: a green cup, a set of sheets, a small pillow, and a wool gray blanket that catches on my skin as soon as it makes contact. "Do I need to change or something?" I ask the inmate.

"No," she says. "You're a detainee. You only get a uniform if you get sentenced." *If you get sentenced.* I have so much to learn about this process.

She and the officer show me to a cell by myself, a cell that's dirty and dark, with one small window facing the shoreline of the Bronx across the East River. Because of the thirty-six hours I spent in police custody without food or anyone to talk to, I fall asleep easily. I'm not sure how long I've been sleeping when I wake up afraid, sweating, breathing heavy because of a nightmare.

They transfer me to a permanent cell by myself at the Rose M. Singer Center, the only facility of the jail that's designated for female inmates. Instinctively, my old childhood habit returns when I check the cell door to see if there's a lock: there's only a lock on the outside of the door, which will give strangers here access to me, but will give me no means to protect myself. Inside the cell is an aluminum toilet, a sink, a metal bed that comes out of the wall with a thin mattress, and a tiny, blocked-up window so that I can't see even the faintest sliver of light. They inform me I'll be allowed out for a maximum of an hour per day.

Meals are delivered to me through a small slot—usually cold, except for the milk or juice, which usually comes warm. Alone in my cell, it begins to physically pain my eyes to see the plastic knives that they give me to cut my food. One of the officers takes me to see the psychiatrist, who suggests that I'm experiencing regressive memories from events that happened in my early childhood. I remember a time when my birth mother held up a knife in the moonlight to a man she was dating, and the way the moon shone off the silver of the knife so sharply that it hurt my eyes.

My nightmares continue, and each night, I wake up in my cell with tears sliding over my jawline, moistening my small square of pillow. In my sleep, I see Roy standing over me, licking his lips and making grunting noises the way he used to do when he insisted that I change my clothes with my bedroom door open. I see my birth mother in Jamaica, screaming and whipping me inside a cave. After a week of this, I call out to one of the correctional officers who walks by my cell. "Can you help me?"

She stops and slowly approaches. "What's the matter?"

"I can't get any sleep. The nightmares—"

"It's OK," she says. "We'll get somebody to help you."

The next morning, she escorts me through the halls of Rikers Island. From inside their cells, I hear women ask each other: "Who is that?" and "Where the fuck does she think she's going?" While we wait to see a doctor who can give me something to help me sleep, the officer asks me whether I have any children. I nod solemnly. "A daughter," I tell her, suddenly forced to fight back tears.

"I'll bet she's beautiful."

I nod and stop a tear with the back of my fist. "I'm sorry."

"That's alright. What's your little girl's name?"

I take a deep breath to catch myself from sobbing. "Adrienne."

"And how old?"

"She's four."

"Where is she now?"

"She's with her father. In the Bronx."

"Are you upset because you're worried about her?" I'm overcome with sadness; I can't speak another word. "She's going to be OK, Donna," the officer tells me. "Right now, you have to take care of you."

It is only the rare displays of humanity and care such as this that make it possible to survive in jail. No one comes to see me, though I do have an opportunity to phone Roy and Daphne for twenty minutes each week. I ask them both about Adrienne, and their answers are brief. They inform me that they've thrown out every award, trophy, and piece of identification that bears my name. I understand what this means: I'm dead to them. It's not just because of the crime, either. It's because of that day when I was twelve years old and dared to tell someone outside our home what had been happening inside. From that moment, I became the troublemaker.

When I hang up, the women behind me are surprised I've used so little of my twenty-minute call allowance.

In a cell by myself I'm going crazy, but around others, the danger seems more severe. "Look at her, she's pretty," the other female inmates say for me to hear when I take my free hour in a common area. There we can watch TV or prepare soup, coffee, or tea from the hot water faucet that pipes out from the wall. "She was in the *New York Post*, bet she thinks she's really something special." Others sneer, "Who does this light-skinned bitch think she is?"

I remember the kids in my class when I was a little girl starting school after I'd just come from Jamaica: *Is she black, or is she white? She's an alien!*

Just as I did back then, I keep to myself here at Rikers. I can tell there are a few who are already out to get me, and my instincts in this place are quickly sharpening. When I've only been here a few days and I'm still getting acquainted, I see motion in my peripheral vision. Something in my mind says, *Stop her!*

I put out my arm and turn just in time to block a woman who was about to splash scalding water in my face. Just as I had to do at seven years old, I need to establish myself at this place as someone they should stay away from. Violence isn't a part of my nature, but here, just like at every other stage in my life, I have to learn whatever it will take to help me survive.

The officers and doctor continue to let me try solutions to help me rest, but sleep only comes for a couple hours at a time at most. My mind turns and turns and turns with memories and anxiety and guilt—with trauma. When I do sleep, Selma has begun to appear to me through the tiny window inside my cell. Even though I know that in real life she'd never be able to fit through that space, her face peaks through and torments my dreams. *Sweetie! Sweetie! What's your name?* If I'd turned and run like my instincts told me to do, things would be so different right now.

As I prepare for my trial, the kind correctional officer continues to look out for me. When my nightmares continue, she convinces one of her colleagues to send me again to the psychiatrist. "I'm going to trial soon," I tell the doctor. "If I don't get some sleep at night, I'm afraid I'll go crazy." He nods and writes out orders, handing them to the officer who will see me back to my cell.

Later that day, another officer brings by a bottle of liquid medicine to my cell. SINEQUAN, it reads. TAKE 150 MILLIGRAMS BY MOUTH, THREE TIMES PER DAY. The taste is bitter, nasty, and the liquid numbs my whole mouth. I begin sleeping more—then too much...and then constantly. Even if I were to call Daphne to find out if there's something better I could take, she wouldn't be willing to talk to me.

After a few weeks in protective custody at Rikers Island, the officers begin to wake me at four o'clock in the morning to leave at 8 a.m. for pretrial hearings, as well as family court. Alvin is officially fighting for full custody of Adrienne, which causes me to fear for my child's life. He is aggressive, impatient, and violent, especially under the pressure of responsibilities. He doesn't have the right demeanor to raise a child, on his own or with anyone else.

The police shuttle me to the Bronx for our hearings where I'm trying to fight for custody so that I can at least have a say in where Adrienne lives. I'm drugged, exhausted, scared, and overwhelmed, and Alvin is so ruthless that my own attorney advises me that continuing to fight isn't likely to get me anywhere. For my daughter, I refuse to give up.

One day in the midst of our battle, Alvin's mother, Dorothy, accepts my call when I phone her. She has always been a supporter for me, as well as a wise and decent woman. She tells me that she promises that if Alvin gets custody, then she, not Alvin, will care for Adrienne. She also pledges that she'll put Adrienne on the phone to speak with me regularly and will bring her to see me for frequent visits, no matter what happens with my trial. If I trust anyone from my past, it's Dorothy. Still, I know Alvin. The sessions at family court continue, and I'm destroyed to learn my attorney was right: it seems I have no choice but to hand Alvin legal custody. Now, nothing about Adrienne's safety is a guarantee. Giving in crushes my heart like a boulder landing on my chest. I have to find some way to continue to push to get her.

Each morning as the pretrial for my criminal case begins, I'm placed in a private holding cell for a few moments before the shuttle arrives to take me to court. There, as I force myself to stay awake, I overhear a conversation between two inmates nearby. "Who's the judge for your case?" one asks.

The other responds: "Rothwax. You know anything about him?"

I do, I think. *He's the judge in my pretrial hearings.*

"Yeah," says the first. "In your cell, do you see a tree out your window?"

"No."

"Don't worry," says the first. "If you get Rothwax, by the time you get out, there will be a full-grown tree there."

I don't know anything about the system, but that doesn't sound good.

The public defender's office assigns a female attorney to my case. She's the first encouraging force I've met since this whole mess started. "Donna, don't worry," she says. "You're going to get out of this. We know you didn't kill anyone."

I nod, so relieved she understands the truth that I want to break down and cry. I see her again at prehearing trials the next day, but then, the following day...I learn that another attorney has taken over my case. From this point, I get another, and then another. Each attorney has a different disposition and varying degrees of interest in learning the details of my case. The problem is further complicated by the fact that ever since I started taking the medicine to try to help me sleep, I can't even stand. In my cell, I try to position myself by the door to listen to what the other inmates say about how to prepare for court and questions we should ask our attorneys, but I can barely keep my head up—the medicine has deadened me and made me confused. I ask a prison officer whether the doctor can permit me not to take the medication, but she says that I have to ask the court to make that decision.

It takes eleven months after the crime for all the pretrial and evidentiary hearings to play out. The attorney who will finally represent me at court is named Richard Siracusa, and I can see that he's committed to my case and doing the best he can for me.

During this time, I learn more about the victim, Thomas Vigliarolo. He was a husband, a father, and a real estate broker who, along with Louis Miranda, allegedly sold shares in NYC condos and pocketed the money. I hear grisly details about what happened inside the apartment that I didn't know because Rita and Theresa often didn't want to speak about it when I returned from driving Miranda around. The other five—Maria, Miranda, Woody, Theresa, and Rita—are named as my co-defendants. My attorney, Richard, asks me whether I want to take a plea bargain of five to fifteen years by confessing to kidnapping. "No," I tell him. "I want to go to trial. I didn't kidnap or murder anyone—I want to tell them the truth!" I don't realize that if the jury should happen to find me guilty, the sentence will be harsher than if I were to take the plea. Selma is the only one of us who's wise enough to the system to accept the plea agreement. She's sentenced with fifteen years to life.

Even though we other six are being tried together, we each have separate attorneys. Richard focuses solely on me, working hard to emphasize the fact that I was an accessory as opposed to someone who planned or willingly participated in any of this. My defense is *duress and coercion*, a phrase I will hear Richard say over and over throughout the trial. He explains that this is when someone is put into a position with imminent threat, participating only due to that threat. Richard tells the court that in fact, it's because of my cooperation that they even found the body of Mr. V, as I've begun to refer to Mr. Vigliarolo in my mind. Mr. V's business partners from Long Island didn't even select me out of the lineup when the investigators asked who delivered the ransom note to them.

Instead, they identified a woman who looked like Maria. Richard points out that I am the only one of us seven who didn't inflict any violence on Mr. V, and after the police took forensic samples of my DNA, I'm also the only one of us seven whose DNA didn't show up anywhere at the scene, and so the authorities could never place me there. Nothing, absolutely nothing—*nothing* came out to prove that I was involved in the murder.

I begin to fear that the court will suspect me of some kind of reverse-lie: I've confessed to being present when Mr. V died, but there's actually no evidence that I was there. It should be easy for Richard to argue for my innocence...shouldn't it?

I'm learning that nothing is sure in court. The judge for my state trial is said to be even harsher than Judge Rothwax: it's Judge Edwin Torres, who wrote the 1979 crime novel *After Hours*. Judge Torres is in his mid-fifties, and everything about him is straightforward and no-nonsense, right down to how tightly he slicks back his hair. I'm intimidated by him, and on the first day of the trial, I throw up right in court. As maintenance workers come in to clean it up during an awkward break from the opening arguments, I keep my head down in humiliation—so out of my element in this world of court and crime. Throughout my whole life, I've never belonged. Can't they see that I don't belong here, either?

"What's the problem with your client?" the judge asks, and Richard explains that I'm on medication to help me sleep. "Take her off!" Judge Torres says angrily. "This is not for this court." He looks at me. "I don't want to see you back like this again."

That afternoon, the court sends me back to Rikers Island with documentation that I'm to be taken off of the Sinequan. "Do you want us to lower the dosage?" the doctor asks me.

"No," I tell him. "I don't want it at all. I've never been on medication. It doesn't agree with me."

Even off of the drug, I'm less in control of my own well-being here at Rikers than I knew. While I've been spending so much time in court, there's a female captain officer at the prison who has grown jealous because her romantic partner, also a female captain, apparently has been showing me favor.

While I'm out, the captain who wants revenge on me enters my cell and hides a straight razor. A short time later, when there's a cell search, officers find the razor in my space. I'm sentenced to the Bing—Rikers Island's nickname for solitary confinement—for sixty days.

With this, and as the trial continues, I'm back to losing sleep. My mind spins with too much anxious activity. These nights, I crave family. I miss my daughter so much I think the longing could kill me. I wish for Dorothy just to show up with her here. I wish I'd had parents like the ones on TV: The Brady Bunch. The Partridge Family. The Cosbys. I know that my parents are never going to care about me, much less love me. I mean nothing to them.

The officer who occasionally asks about Adrienne sees what I'm going through and continues to talk with me, to look in my eyes and see my humanness. One day during my trial, she tells me something that I'll never forget: "You don't deserve to get a lot of time in prison—but don't worry," she says. "You have to have faith that your daughter's going to be alright." Even if neither one of us can know that for sure, it brings me some relief to hear someone say it. Maybe I'm really not such a bad person if this person cares enough to offer me some encouragement in my struggle.

I pray that the court and jury will see things the same way. My trial begins in February 1986, just a couple of weeks after Adrienne's fifth birthday. The forewoman of the jury is a black woman who asks a lot of intelligent questions about the circumstances and the evidence.

Into the microphone, I tell the jury my truth. I tell the court what happened, and why: that under threat of my daughter's life, I did what they told me to do. I acknowledge that I made a mistake by agreeing to a blackmail scheme, even though I didn't understand at all that's what it was. I tell them that Mr. V asked me to help him...and that I wanted to help him. I just didn't know how to do that without putting my life and my daughter's life in danger.

With each testimony, the trial grows more complicated. Rita and Theresa both testify against me, and some of my co-defendants' testimonies conflict with the forensic results of the investigation. The one person who tries to help me during recesses and back at Rikers Island is Sr. Elinor, a Catholic nun who works in a program called the Women's Advocate Ministry, visiting people in prison to advocate for legal justice on their behalf. She's a strong source of support for me, and I appreciate the time and insights she gives me. I need any advocate I can get.

"Tell me about your childhood," Sr. Elinor says. I hold back momentarily, not wanting any part of the trial to be about me. It's Mr. V whose life deserves the attention. But Sr. Elinor explains that there's a small chance this could help my case, so I begin to share some stories about my upbringing with her. I tell her about my mother in Jamaica and how I ended up in New York. We discuss Roy, why he might have treated me the way that he did... but that's a question I'll never be able to answer. There's so much about Roy that's a mystery. For the seven years I lived in their home, I knew very little about him and Daphne on a personal level. I offer Sr. Elinor the relatively sparse background about my adoptive father that I did learn over the years: I remember hearing when I was little that Roy was always different than the other children in his family, but I never found out what that meant. He once told me he served in the Korean War, but his older age leads me to believe that it was actually World War II. At times when I was very small, I would ask him his age, but he would never tell—he was very self-conscious about growing old. When he did talk about fighting at war, he told me that they would experiment with gasses on people. I've begun to think maybe that led to his mental instability.

He once shared with me that he believes he fathered a son with a German woman while he served in the war, which may also solidly support that it was not the Korean War he was part of. He said he never found out for sure whether she bore his child—but by the look on his face as he spoke about it, I could tell that deep down, he knew. "Don't ever tell your mother I told you that," he said. "She doesn't know." Daphne wasn't able to have children, and I remember learning that only by chance. Otherwise it was a forbidden discussion. Daphne was ashamed of failure in any form—especially one so quintessential to the experience of womanhood.

Just as I did with the police following Mr. V's death, I volunteer everything I know to Sr. Elinor in the event it could help my case. She relays information about my upbringing to Richard, my attorney, and encourages him to ask for the judge's allowance to listen to background about my life. "Donna ran away from home at age fourteen for a reason," Sr. Elinor reminds Richard. In turn, he tries to reason with Judge Torres, but the judge decides he won't allow my personal history to be heard in the court.

During the trial process, the only other opportunity to share anything about my life takes place with the probation officer who's working to prepare my presentence report. "Where were you born?" the probation officer asks me.

"Jamaica."

"Jamaica, Queens?"

"No. Jamaica, West Indies."

I notice that he writes the word *allegedly* to state my birthplace as Jamaica. Unfortunately, the only person in the world who has any record to prove my adoption from Jamaica is Roy Hylton. "What is this for?" I ask the probation officer.

"This is a report of a defendant's personal history that the judge is supposed to take into consideration when they're weighing the severity of the defendant's sentence. And from now on, I ask the questions. You answer. You got it?"

I lower my eyes.

There's a small handful of people connected to the case who tell the truth on the stand with sincerity. One of them is the waitress from the donut shop near Maria's apartment. Another is a Nassau County police officer who drove me around after we were arrested. He tells the court that I was cooperative in assisting the police with information about the crime and says I was in over my head, not knowing whom to trust. On the stand, he states he doesn't feel as though I should be blamed for all this—I didn't even know the victim.

From start to finish, the trial continues for a month. On Wednesday, March 12, 1986—three hundred fifty-seven days after I first encountered Mr. V—the jury steps out of the courtroom to deliberate the verdict.

After many hours, they all file back into the courtroom. The forewoman explains that they have a strong consensus, but there are a couple of charges that they need the judge to clarify. "Could you again define duress and coercion?" she asks. Members of the jury look at me with a softness in their eyes. They seem to know that I was an accessory, and not an active participant. I agreed to a blackmail scheme, but I didn't agree to anything else that happened. As I look around, I sense a feeling in the courtroom that we three girls didn't intend to be part of Mr. V's death. We were caught up in something we could not get out of.

Two more times, the jury leaves and reenters the courtroom for further clarification. *Does this mean that they're not all in agreement about my involvement? Please, let them understand the charges and know that I'm not guilty of murder.*

But finally, for a fourth time, they reenter the courtroom and take their seats in the jury box. The forewoman looks pained. She grips the wooden ledge of the jury box in front of her as she rises to read the verdict:

"On two counts of kidnapping in the first degree, Donna Hylton has been found...guilty."

The room begins to swirl around me.

The forewoman continues:

"On one count of murder in the second degree, Donna Hylton has been found—"

I hold my breath—

"Guilty."

What? I'm confused. In the moment, I'm present, but the dissociation comes quickly. I go numb—not numb without feeling, but numb with too much feeling. *I didn't kill Mr. V.*

And then the second voice enters my consciousness: *But you didn't help him, either.*

The verdicts of the other five are read, but the high sonic tone of shock continues to ring between my ears, deafening me against everything that's happening around me.

Later, when I learn the verdicts of the others, I find that we've all been charged the same. The technicality is that Mr. V died during the act of kidnapping, which was a felony, and this is considered murder. When we receive our sentences, I learn that every single one of us has gotten twenty-five years to life. If I'd never said I was there, they wouldn't have had any evidence to place me at the scene. It's because I told the truth that I'm being convicted.

Twenty-five years to life. I'm twenty-one years old, and my life is over.

I don't know yet that I'm about to discover real love, purpose, and strength for the first time in my life... and that the only person I've ever needed to learn to save is myself.

4

INMATE #86G0206

Outside the courthouse as cameras snap and reporters shout their questions, Judge Torres refers to Mr. V's death as "the crime of the century." This will do all the more to bring me unwanted attention in the headlines, as well as in prison itself.

My new home will be the Bedford Hills Correctional Facility, the nation's only maximum-security prison for women and known at Rikers Island as "Beddy's House"—as in, "Look out: When you get to Beddy's House, they rape you. They beat you up; they take your stuff from the commissary. You end up at Beddy's House? Then you gotta be real careful."

Two police vehicles escort the New York City van in which I'm transported an hour outside of the city to a facility with towers, fences, and barbed wires. As we pull inside the prison gates, some incarcerated women come out and stand behind the chain-link fences, watching the show as I'm ushered out of the vehicle in handcuffs. I've worn an outfit that a friend bought me—a little pale baby-yellow blouse and matching cotton capris with sandals. In my ears are tiny diamond studs, on my wrist, a small watch. I'm the only one who's dressed in normal clothes...and because of this, as usual, I don't fit in.

I subtly scan the crowd to see if I recognize anyone who might have been at Rikers Island with me. There's not a familiar face among these women.

Twenty-five years to life, I think again. I've done the multiplication: that's 9,130 days, counting leap years. *When will Dorothy bring Adrienne to see me?*

I'm taken into the reception building, where immediately one of the inmates working there takes me to shower with lye to treat any possible lice. The women instruct me to shampoo my hair, again on both areas of my body, and wash with the soap that they give me. "This soap takes scars away if you use it long enough," one tells me. *You don't know my scars,* I'm tempted to tell her.

Only a thin prison robe separates me from the cold bench, as I wait for officers to look me up and down and tell me what I'll wear. I've heard that state greens are made for men, by men, to fit men, and that rolling the waistline of the pants down to make them fit can get you in trouble. Fortunately, they give me a green prison dress, which fits alright, at least for now. They also allow me to keep my own shoes on, since they're sandals.

As I dress, I think of all the years I looked forward to choosing my own clothes, all the times when Daphne dressed me like a miniature professor and my shoulders sagged under the weight of her rule. The clothes we wear are an expression of the way we feel inside. Now, anything that ever made me an individual is taken away. This moment feels exactly the way I felt when I was seven years old, moving into the Hyltons' home. As a child in Jamaica, I was on my own so often that I never had to fight to cultivate a sense of who I was—a child who was carefree and happy, who loved the water and the birds and the butterflies. Despite the lack of consistent parenting, I inherently understood my connection with God—that I was lovable, that I was loved... that I was love itself.

But in time, that inherent understanding diffused and eventually disappeared. I became nobody, not important to anybody. And now, that understanding is reinforced. I'm one of four hundred women in this place who has to follow other people's rules. Right now I'm angry—at my co-defendants, at the people who never believed me when I tried to speak the truth, but mostly, at myself. Mr. V's life has ended, but so has his family's life, along with my daughter's, along with mine. The worst part of all of this is that despite Dorothy's promise, I really *don't* know when I'll ever get to see Adrienne. Alvin has a way of manipulating every situation and every person, including his mother.

If I had any sense of personhood left before I entered, any ability to manage the things in my life that are most important to me, that's all gone now. I'm a ward of the state, deemed as unfit for making decisions for my life. From now on, the State of New York will determine what happens to me. I have to conform to everything that's expected of every other individual in here.

For twenty-five years to life.

I work to adapt to the routines at Bedford Hills, hoping my baggy greens will help me blend in with the other women. Even though the correction officers conduct four body counts per day to keep constant track of where every single one of us is, I feel lost and invisible. Every morning, the doors of my cell spring open at 6 a.m., and every night they slam shut with a thunderous *clang* at 10 p.m. I'm trapped, smothered inside a metal coffin. Imagining years upon years of this makes me scream inside.

I squint up at the tiny window in my cell to find some hope of life outside, but I can barely find a patch of sky. Mr. V twists my thoughts, visits my dreams and doesn't let up, begging me with pleading eyes: "You're different. Will you help me?"

Look at me, Mr. V! I can't even help myself!

I'm also haunted incessantly by agonizing worries about my little girl. The one solace, the little piece of hope that I cling to, is of one day seeing Adrienne, and the dream that prison will not be where I will live the rest of my life. I pray that I'll get out, and Adrienne and I will have a home together.

Night after night, sometimes multiple times in one night, I wake up with dreams that now consist of events that I've forgotten. After finding a caterpillar in my salad in the mess hall one evening, I've stopped eating. My stomach rumbles in hunger through the night, and for the first time in years, I'm left alone with moments from my childhood that are surfacing out of nowhere. As if it happened yesterday, I remember how my birth mother loved to prepare big breakfasts and dinners. I remember how she would hum as she stood over the stove to whatever songs played on the jukebox at the pub or through the radio in our home and from the street vendors: songs like "No Woman, No Cry" by Bob Marley, Dennis Brown's "No Man Is an Island," and "The Harder They Come" by Jimmy Cliff.

And then I remember something I haven't thought of since around the time I came to the United States. One day, my birth mother took me to visit a mansion on a bluff overlooking the sea. She held my hand as we approached the house with its white pillars, walking carefully past two big dogs sitting like sentries outside. A black maid opened the front door and stared at me with pity in her eyes. "Come in, child," she said, watching my mother closely as I walked with dirty feet across the polished wood foyer floor. The maid went to fetch my mummy's boss, whose hurried expression softened when he looked out from his library to see us. He went back inside his library, and then a minute later emerged to hand my mother a piece of paper. Then he knelt down to look me in the eye, placing his hand gently on my shoulder. "I'm sorry that I haven't been here," he told me, "and that I haven't seen you."

All I've ever known about this man is his name, and that during my childhood, he was an attorney who employed my mother. At this point, I crave connection so acutely that I decide I'll reach out to anyone in my past who cared about me, for a chance they'll help me stay connected to what's going on in the outside world.

Another inmate's daughter is said to have a knack for locating long-lost relatives, and within a few weeks, she's been able to find the phone number for the law office of my mother's long-ago employer. Because the number is long-distance, an inmate arranges for us to have a three-way phone call—a violation in the prison, but one that I'm desperate enough to risk. When I hear a man's British-Jamaican accent come on the line, my voice is as small as a child's. "Mr. James Adamson?"

"Yes?"

"My name is Donna. My mother worked for you in the early sixties as a secretary...and she used to bring me there as a child..."

With every detail, he responds, "Yes...yes...?"

I recall to him a time when I was a toddler accompanying my mother to his home. The vision is still vivid: the waves that washed up at the bottom of the cliff behind the mansion, its massive pillars out front, the dogs that stood guard beneath the veranda. "Yes..." he says.

I've never forgotten thinking back then how strange it was that my mother's boss would relate to me so personally, but in the years since, I think maybe I've put it together. Now, twenty years later and two thousand miles away, I ask him: "Mr. Adamson...am I your daughter?"

He's so quiet on the other line that for a moment I'm sure the line's been cut off. But then, he answers with a stutter: "I...I don't—no!" he exclaims. "You are *not* my daughter!"

I'm left with a dead tone on the line.

If no one wants you, then you belong to no one. You fit in

nowhere. In the bottom of my heart, I'd begun to grip this hope like a tiny fistful of sand. *Maybe if he knew how badly I've been harmed, he would come straight here and save me. Could James Adamson be my father?*

I think of everything I'd do for Adrienne—the only person in the world who really loves me.

I begin to accept with gratitude any opportunity for connection, eventually finding companionship with a woman named Yolanda, known here as "Ya-Ya," who's in for assault and selling drugs. I don't consider myself gay, but at a certain point, prison makes you desperate for friendship, love, protection, and above all else, it makes you desperate to feel something—*anything*—that's life-affirming and human. Ya-Ya and I begin to meet in the recreation yard and the gym, where we sing together and steal kisses.

Unfortunately, this newfound security soon becomes a problem. Ya-Ya is young, fun, good-looking, and gay. And she has an admirer—an ogre of a woman who's known to be a fighter and who confronts me one afternoon during recreation break in the yard. "Uh-oh," one of the women says to me, her eyes monitoring something over my shoulder. "It looks like somebody's coming for you."

I turn to find Ursula towering over me. When we're nose to nose, I realize I've never seen her this close: the scars on her face, her bloodshot eyes, her jaw clamped in aggression. I square my shoulders, trying to look brave... and in response, Ursula breaks into crazy laughter. Just as she pulls her chin back to spit on me, I clench my fist tight, haul it back, and nail her—hard.

She falls onto her knees and grips the side of her head with both hands, then pulls one away and looks at it: there's blood. In this instant, I'm staring at Roy's clawed cheek in my bedroom back at Boynton the day that I went to the school counselor for help. *You made me bleed, you little bitch!*

She looks up at me with crazy eyes, and suddenly I'm filled with all the strength I lost in the decade and a half of my life since Roy began to molest me. My body spews rage as I rail on Ursula, fighting like I've never fought before, until my fist loosens enough for her to catch part of my hand in her mouth. The jaggedness of her broken teeth locks around my finger, which is quickly going purple with pressure. An officer races toward us from the reception building, followed by several others, who work to yank me off of her and put cuffs on us both. Several of them escort me immediately to see the doctor, who advises me that I'll require a tetanus shot.

"I think it'll heal on its own, though," I tell him.

The doctor turns to me. "Your opponent in the fight has a virus that's very serious, and very contagious," he says.

"How serious?"

"Deadly." My stomach collapses. "We don't know whether it can be passed on through saliva, but I believe this shot is the least we should do. It's not worth taking a chance."

I turn the top of my forearm to him. My mind aches with worry about the virus he mentioned for weeks longer than it takes the pain of the tetanus shot to leave my arm.

At the disciplinary hearing they hold, Ursula cradles the side of her head in pain as I learn that I busted her eardrum with my punch. It was a means not to allow myself to appear weak here, but I'm learning that in prison, the truth doesn't matter so much. The system on the inside is a lot like the system on the outside: unless you have a good ally in a powerful position to speak up for you, you're at its mercy. At Bedford, like at Boynton and in every place in my life, it doesn't matter that I was simply trying to stand up for myself.

It's here, less than a year into my sentence, that I'm locked up for the first time in the SHU—segregated housing unit—better known as solitary, or, as the women here call it…the Box. As I enter the Box for a sentence of three years, my relationship with Ya-Ya extinguishes…and I'm disturbingly aware that the next 1,095 days will be the loneliest period I have faced so far. The only interaction I have with another human is the gloved hand that passes me moldy bread and spoiled milk through a slot in the steel door, and as I look around at the six-foot-by-ten-foot cinder block room with a slab of metal for a bed and no clock to tell me the time, I face my worst nightmare: myself, my memories, and my mind.

Going to the Box is like being buried alive in a coffin within a coffin. This is the pinnacle of all the anxiety, loneliness, and dark closets I've experienced in my life. I've heard of women who have hung themselves with bedsheets while they were in the Box.

This I don't know if I can survive.

5

JAIL SISTERS

I hear screams coming from the other boxes, and I scream out, too. Even in summer, this place is an icebox, and there are dozens of tiny black bugs that scatter among each other on the window with no rhythm or pattern. The longer I watch them, the less sure I am that they actually exist. Even in the first few days here, I'm sure I'm losing my mind.

When an officer pulls me out for my first chance to spend an hour in recreation, I look into the window of the cell that neighbors mine. Lying on her metal bed is a small, white woman who's reading a book, which she slowly moves away from her face, perhaps as curious about her new neighbor as I am about mine. Our eyes meet. *Oh, no. Here's what I get for not minding my own business.* Before the officer moves me along, this neighbor's face softens...and opens into a big smile.

From this point, every time I'm escorted past her cell, she takes a moment's break from reading to smile at me.

The screams and cries might happen more sparsely in the night, but they never fully stop. Segregated housing is a prison of the self and of the system. On the occasion when the self softens enough to ask for mercy from its pain, the system never forgives or forgets. One night, in this dismal hellhole, I hear a voice: "Hello? Are you there?"

I rise briskly from my bed, scared that I'm hallucinating. As I move to the wall, as if it could somehow defend me from insanity, I hear it again: the voice coming from an air vent. Slowly, I move underneath it. "Hello?" I ask softly.

"Hi, I'm Judy—Judy Clark."

I have no idea who she is, but this connection feels like it was sent from God. From the first moment I saw her smile, and now as I hear her voice, it's been clear that Judy's presence might be the only thing to get me through prison.

Some days, we're allowed to go to our one-hour recreation together, where we walk along the paved asphalt area—twenty feet by twenty feet, with two concrete tables, a barbed razor-wire fence, and a gun tower. This space is even higher security than the rest of the jail, but as I spend time with Judy, my anguish to get out of this place somehow lessens in urgency. Before I came to segregated housing, I heard her name mentioned around the prison—she's one of the higher-profile women at Bedford. Women seemed to talk about her with appreciation, but as young and new as I was, I didn't really get why she mattered.

Now, as Judy and I spend time together each day, I'm beginning to learn why she's widely known, not only here but in larger
society. Raised by parents who were part of the American Com-
munist Party, Judy was a passionate political activist in the civil
rights and women's liberation movements. Along with another
incarcerated woman here named Kathy Boudin, Judy participated
in the radical political activist group called the Weather Underground Organization. Throughout the sixties and seventies, they
worked with extremist groups that included the Black Panther
Party and the Black Liberation Army. Judy was captured during
the infamous Brink's robbery of 1981 that left two police officers
and two security guards dead. She was sentenced to prison because
she was part of a movement that challenged the injustices happening against women and people of color. It's easy to witness Judy's
commitment to creating a more just world for everyone. While she
denounced the way some humans treat one another, she's stated
that she has regrets for the role she played in her crime. Judy Clark
might be locked up in prison, but she tells me she still feels the
responsibility to do *something*.

On days when our recreation breaks take place at different
times, we talk for hours through the wall vent that separates our
cells. She starts out curious about my age, where I'm from, whether
I keep in touch with my family. As our conversations through the
vent progress, I learn that Judy and I both have daughters who
are in first grade. When Judy was arrested, she said goodbye to an
infant. I listen, in awe of her strength. When I tell her that I had
my daughter at age sixteen by an older man, even though there's a

thick cement division between us, I can feel that she sympathizes with me.

Judy tells me she's doing her best to parent from prison, but she faces her most difficult challenge every time she has to say goodbye to her daughter. "I feel like I'm no good," I tell her. "I can't even see or hold my little girl, and I definitely don't think I'm doing a good job of parenting her from inside this place."

"Can I tell you something?" she says.

I rest my head on the wall under the vent to listen.

As though she can sense this, Judy tells me: "Just loving your daughter is parenting."

The safety of her friendship seems to allow more memories that I'd buried to surface. For the first time in more than fifteen years, I remember a teenage girl who came to live with me at Roy and Daphne's home shortly after I arrived there. For a short time, maybe a few months, I had a companion to eat dinner with me in the shush of the evening and someone who was allowed to take me to the playground or to walk down the block.

And I remember that she left suddenly, which disappointed me. When I asked Roy and Daphne why, they told me she decided to go away to the army. She was a beautiful, delicate type, and for the first time it seems glaringly obvious to me why she really would have left. She probably couldn't stand life with Roy.

When she hears a little about my past, Judy emphasizes to me that even though I'm in prison, I need to continue to learn, to keep my mind busy. At rec, she passes books to me and encourages me to share my thoughts and opinions with her about what I've read. There's so much screaming and discord in our unit that Judy becomes a safe place for me.

With her friendship and wisdom, I'm able to keep my mind occupied in a positive way. I'd never met anyone like Judy on the outside—so passionate and effective in activating change in the world. She becomes the first of many role models that I'll meet in prison who will stir my mind and spur me to use my brain for something positive for the first time since I earned my GED.

And so it begins, the point where my prison experience has an unexpected and profound effect in transforming who I am. Following a past in which my decisions, my judgment, and my actions hurt people, this relationship will be the first torch in the darkness that will light the way to my redemption. It's inside the Box, at the most isolated moment of my life, that I begin to find sisterhood and community.

The emotional resources that I'm learning to cultivate here, like Judy's encouragement about parenting, become especially important in mid-1988, when after ten months I'm released from the Box. This is when I finally get an opportunity to attend a family court hearing to fight for visits with Adrienne. This will be the first time in two years that I've gotten to see my daughter, who's now seven years old.

In leg irons and handcuffs, I'm led into the courtroom to try to work out my visitation rights—

And that's when I see her.

In blue jeans and a T-shirt, Adrienne stands next to Alvin. I have to catch myself from breaking down in tears as I notice the most basic of details: her hair is falling out of her ponytail. It's a symbol of a little girl's natural, carefree innocence, but in Adrienne's case I fear it may be a sign of her father's negligence. As officers walk me down the center aisle of the courtroom, it stabs me in the heart to walk her way without the ability to touch her. My little girl stares at the ground until I walk by—when she turns her head just slightly in my direction.

She's the same age I was when my mother gave me to the Hyltons. I would never have made a conscious decision to let someone else have my daughter, and I know the peril of a child's future if she doesn't have her mother to nurture her, to praise her, to cry to, to count on. It takes every cell inside me not to fall to the ground and beg the court to let her come with me.

As I take my place at the podium, I have to lean for emotional strength onto another resource I've learned is available for incarcerated women: a Catholic nun named Sr. Elaine. She's accompanied me to court as an advocate who works to keep families in close contact after the mother has been incarcerated. With her skilled understanding of the law, Sr. Elaine has prepared me for court and written a letter to the judge to state that since I entered prison, my daughter's father has not complied per the visitation rights that the court granted me. "When you went to prison," Sr. Elaine has explained to me, "you didn't give up your rights as a mother." She explains that unless Alvin brings Adrienne to see me, he'll be in contempt of court.

Alvin challenges the judge with defiance and tells the court I'm a bad mother. When the judge directs a few brief questions to

Adrienne, she keeps her head down and only responds with nods or shakes of her head. I can't tell whether she's angry with me, or whether Alvin has primed her with what to say with the threat of beating her. The only thing that's clear from my daughter's behavior is that this whole ordeal has hurt her deeply.

This is all your fault, Donna.

The court orders that Alvin begin to bring Adrienne to visit me twice a month. Sr. Elaine grips my hand in victory, but as I watch Adrienne exit the courtroom next to her father, this outcome has only stirred a different worry in me. It's likely Adrienne will take the brunt of Alvin's defeat. When he's not in control, he turns vicious.

When the date for our first visit arrives the following weekend, neither Alvin nor Adrienne show. I contact Dalida, my former manager from the gift shop at the Milford Plaza, who has graciously kept in contact with me. She goes out on a search for my daughter and informs me weeks later that Alvin had moved without formally changing his address. She found Adrienne near her school in the Bronx, hungry, scratching at the lice in her hair, looking for ways to earn money to eat.

As my mind leaps into crisis mode, I relay this information to Sr. Elaine, who quickly writes a letter to the court and goes to a hearing for me. Her advocacy on my behalf shows me that there are ways I can grow more empowered if I have an understanding of the law and my rights.

Having experienced a sense of camaraderie and support for the first time, I feel determined to seek out Judy's contemporary, Kathy

Boudin, as well as any other women who can guide me. I want to begin to build a family around myself—not a family who makes me earn their love, the way I had to do as a child, but a family who will foster my heart as well as the growth of my learning and my peace of mind for my daughter. When I first entered prison, I couldn't even get my mind around the magnitude of *twenty-five years to life*. Now, as I begin to deal with the realities of life in prison, I know that I need to learn how not to be that isolated little girl. I need to find a group of women who can provide wisdom and support to help me navigate this life emotionally, psychologically, spiritually, and legally.

As I engage with more of the women, I begin to understand the kind of place Bedford Hills Correctional Facility for Women is. Bedford houses some of the most infamous female convicts whose crimes took place in New York State. There's Jean Harris, once a prominent boarding school administrator who was convicted of second-degree murder for the 1981 death of her ex-lover, Dr. Herman Tarnower, author of the best-selling *The Complete Scarsdale Medical Diet*. There's also Elaine Bartlett, who was sentenced to twenty-five years to life for a first-time drug offense of selling cocaine (and who now is fighting for her release to get back to her children), as well as Betty Gal Tyson, a former prostitute from Rochester who was convicted of murdering one of her clients, who was an executive at Kodak.

By the time I arrived at Bedford, Betty was the longest-serving woman at Bedford and regarded as the Mother of the prison. I first encountered her in the rec yard shortly after I arrived from Rikers

Island, and I heard that she was known outside as a "cold-blooded killer." But right away, my perception of her was nothing like that. The first time I saw her in the yard, Betty Tyson was impossible not to notice. She walked tall, her long, shapely legs rising out of red high heels. *How does she get away with those?* I wondered, continuing to take her in. Her skin was dark brown and so smooth that it glowed, her hair long dreadlocks that coiled into a neat bun at the crown of her head. I was drawn in by her dress and appearance, polished and beautiful from head to toe.

Now that I've been released from the Box, Betty Tyson and I are housed on the east wing of the prison, where in the kitchenette she cooks small meals from things she buys in the commissary. One night, she invites me to join her for dinner, and as we talk quietly, she sees something in me—my young age, perhaps, or maybe it's my quiet nature—and she promises to look out for me. We begin to eat like this together. Most every night, Betty uses these meals as opportunities to advise me on how to speak to the correctional officers and the administrators in the prison. Out in the rec yard, she introduces me to people I need to know. This is an invaluable gesture that helps me feel a little more included, as an introduction from Betty means you're "good people," part of the "in" crowd—finally.

As I get to know her, I'm seeing that her beauty and the power of her influence at Bedford radiate from inside of her. She has a way of commanding respect from both the women and the staff that I never would have known was possible—not like the respect on the prison TV shows and movies I watched as a child, which was based in fear. The respect that Betty attracts is based in love. She's very maternal, warm, and comforting. This is a quality that I've longed to find in someone since my early childhood.

She seems to recognize this desire in me, my trust and vulnerability, the same way that I recognize her strength. But she doesn't use this pureness about me against me, as so many in my past have done. Instead, she gently takes me under her wing. While most of the women here call her "Ms. Tyson" or "Nanny," after close to a year of living on the same unit, Ms. Tyson tells me: "You can call me 'Mom.' "

My heart soars with happiness. No one has ever in my life embraced me like this before. For me it's an honor to be one of her "own." Mom opens up to me about the crime she was convicted of, never wavering that she was innocent. She admits that she was indeed a prostitute, but that she didn't kill the man she's been accused of killing. She says she feels she was targeted for the conviction because of the way she made a living—but that she wasn't the one who killed him.

My prison mother is working to create an outward security for me here, but I don't know if she's aware that when she shares with me her own experience with our justice system, she's helping me establish a certain security within myself, also. In just the short time I've been at Bedford, I've listened to the ways women talk about how they got here. Some, like Judy, completely own the part they played in a crime. Others, like Betty Gal Tyson, hold steadfastly to their innocence. In both cases, and even among women whose guilt or innocence is less black and white, there's a personal strength, a commitment to self, that comes from bearing witness to the *truth* of the events that brought them here. As citizens—defendants—and now as incarcerated women, we might have no control over the court's decision to have sentenced us here...but we do have power over our response to it, and who we choose to be while we're in this place.

I continue to observe some of the better-known women here. Judy Clark's one-time co-defendant, Kathy Boudin, often sits on the ground during recreation, singing while she plays her guitar. Women gather around her, sitting and listening, and Kathy utilizes these gatherings as an opportunity to discuss the issues that are happening in the prison. I'm seeing how genuine passion gives way to a generosity of spirit that truly sparks the possibility to create change, and how even inside prison, it's possible—maybe even necessary—to decide on something we believe in, and stand for it.

The friendships I make during these first years at Bedford begin to have a profound effect on me. I'm learning what true friendship is, and what it is to have a stable support system for the first time in my life. These women become the basis, the womb, from which my rebirth will come.

6

AGENTS OF CHANGE

My experience among some of the strongest women at Bedford will give me the example I need to involve myself in the first of several causes that I'll begin to fight for. By now, in the late 1980s, a mysterious illness has begun to hit our facility strongly—the same illness I'd been warned about after my altercation with Ursula. There are some women who are locked in for the nighttime count, but the next morning, they don't wake up because they've died during the night. There are three or four of these deaths each week, and the prison staff won't open up about what's happening.

We women, on the other hand, are talking. The illness is called HIV, or human immunodeficiency virus, in which the body attacks its own immune system. In its final stages, HIV is referred to as AIDS, or autoimmune deficiency syndrome.

It so happens that in my wing, I've met a young woman named

Helen who's in for attempted murder and prostitution. I've learned that these two crimes too often go hand in hand: by the time a woman is in a position to sell her body for money, she's so vulnerable to abuse that she could easily end up dead. Often, to make it out of a situation alive, she has to kill the man who's paid for her services or the one who's selling her body.

Because I know sexual trauma personally, I can sense this experience in Helen. She tends to keep to herself and protect herself from interactions with others. As I continue to push myself beyond the comforts of my own introversion, I try to strike up conversations with her. She has trouble looking in my eyes, but I can tell she appreciates my effort from the hint of a smile she gives me. I try to include her in conversations and activities with the other women, until I notice that for a couple of days, she hasn't left her cell. "Where's Helen?" I ask a few of the women in our unit.

They shrug. "She won't come out," one of them says. "An officer said she's too sick to eat."

"Does anybody want to check on her?" asks a nearby officer.

"*I'm* not going," some of the women say. Something about it reminds me of the time I wanted to feed Mr. V, when Maria told me: "*I'm* not gonna feed him."

"I'll go." Helen's cell is near the unit door opening, cracked ever so slightly partway—almost as though she's inviting one of us to take enough initiative to check in on her. I pull the door farther open, and there I find her: Helen is curled up, in a fetal position on her bed. Again, the feeling of this takes me back to my experience with Mr. V and reminds me of the very thin line between life and death when I realize that I can't tell if Helen is breathing.

My first reaction is a panicked anger: *Why hasn't anyone checked on her?!*

But I pause for a moment and remember what I've learned here: I can choose my response. I can choose to do what's right. In this moment, I choose compassion.

As I enter Helen's cell, some of the women in our unit begin to gather outside the door. "No, no, don't go in there," a few of them say. "She has that thing! You'll catch it from her!"

I walk to her bed and lean over her. "Helen?" She blinks weakly.

I rest my hand on her forehead—she's burning up, clammy and hot.

Oh my God.

I take a washcloth from the small stack of linens in her room and push the cold water pedal on the floor next to her sink to moisten the washcloth. I return to her and wipe her forehead, wipe her face, wipe her neck and chest, trying to give her some relief. She blinks again, faintly, but as if to say: *Thank you, Donna.*

I step out to the crowd in the corridor, which now includes the officer on duty in our unit. "She needs help. Everybody—she fucking needs help!"

They look at each other, not knowing what to do.

I march back inside Helen's cell, where I spot a small carton of juice. I drop the straw that's lying next to it inside the carton, and place it to her lips. Slowly, gently, she sips. After she's taken a few drinks and signals *No more* with her face, like a baby learning to eat, I pick her up. "Where are you going?" the corrections officer asks me.

"I'm taking her to the hospital, that's where I'm going. You're not helping her, but I'm going to help her. Somebody's going to see her."

This most urgent situation becomes my initiation into the rest of my life.

As angry as I am at the corrections officer and the other women for the way they judged Helen, I'm thankful—thankful that for the first time, I had the strength to stand up and say: *This is not right!* I wasn't able to do that for Mr. V, and I've regretted it and blamed myself every day since. In a certain sense, regret is the same as judgment or a lack of forgiveness: a disempowering feeling that we have no control over something that took place before the present moment. This pain I've carried since that day in April 1985 is enough. I can never let that happen again.

As I watch the nurses transfer her to a bed, take her vitals, and connect her with IVs, it begins to dawn on me how fear and ignorance cause us to lose our compassion. We label other people, dehumanize them, slander them when what they need is our love. So many of us here know it very personally: without love, we can't survive.

I spend days on work detail and my nights visiting Helen until she's released from the hospital and housed back in her cell. I buy food from the commissary and cook for her. I clean her living space so that she can rest peacefully there. During recreation, I take her to get fresh air outside, where we play cards and listen to Kathy Boudin sing along with her guitar. Helen visibly relaxes to the sound of the strumming, and when she laughs, it floods my heart with profound satisfaction. On the rare occasion she forgets the shame of her life long enough to allow her eyes to meet mine, I hear Mr. V's words to me from that half-decade ago:

You're different than the others.

After the agonies I've been through, witnessing the way life shines through Helen gives me something I can only describe as spiritual fulfillment. During this season of my friend's life, I discover a new way to experience the world and the inexplicable healing of the self that emerges from the act of serving others. After all my years trying to escape my reality in one way or another, I've found a way that's real and meaningful to truly get out of my misery. That way is simply to help someone else.

After about a year since that day I found her curled up and alone inside her cell, it's clear that Helen's time with us is approaching its end. She's housed in the hospice unit of the prison, where I care for her each day until it's time for me to report back to my cell for the nightly lock-in. "I love you like a sister," Helen tells me one evening.

I kiss her forehead and squeeze her hand. "I love you, too. Now you try to get some sleep."

The next morning when I return, one of the nurses meets me. Her face is sullen—she doesn't have to tell me the news.

"Can I see her?" I ask.

In sadness, she shakes her head no. "They've already taken her body, Donna."

I stare, blankly. *She won't suffer anymore.*

But I'm never going to see Helen again.

After her body is laid to rest, we hold a memorial for her at the prison. I play a cassette of Helen's favorite song: the Stephanie Mills version of "Home," from the original Broadway cast of the musical *The Wiz*:

> *When I think of home, I think of a place*
> *Where there's love overflowing...*

I scan the faces among our group of women—several here who had once turned their backs on Helen. Now they stand for her, in tears. The realization breaks open within me that it is in the most difficult moments in life that humans realize how much we truly have in common with each other. Not one of us here hasn't known the rejection, shame, and loneliness that Helen lived with every day of her life. There are moments during the memorial service for Helen when for the first time, I'm able to hold my shoulders high—not out of pride or righteousness, but out of certainty that I did the best I could for someone who needed me.

As we enter the nineties, Helen's death and the deaths of so many other women at Bedford begin to have a true and transformative effect on some of us. I don't want anything about my experience in prison to begin to feel comfortable, or even normal. In the days and weeks following Helen's passing, what I've begun to learn from Judy and Kathy resonates in my mind: Helen proved to us that there's real work to do. HIV and AIDS are *happening*. Even the toughest among us are scared. While there are women here suffering, the rest of us need to *do* something.

The prison superintendent, Elaine Lord, emerges as one of the very first female authority figures whom I can trust enough to respect when she notes the need for understanding in the prison about the illness. She allows Judy Clark, Kathy Boudin, a few others, and me to create what we call an AIDS Counseling and Education program, which we come to refer to as "ACE." We receive training to provide peer counseling to other women in the prison who may be considering getting tested for HIV, as well as training to educate our fellow incarcerated women about the illness. We also make ourselves available to go along with them for testing so that they won't be alone. Then we provide support while they wait for the results, which makes for a few weeks fraught with worry. Our motto is: "If you're infected, we're all affected." No matter what any of the women have done or experienced, we're by their side to provide comfort and information.

Superintendent Lord is a believer in tough love—she was one of the administrators who sentenced me to the Box for my conflict with Ursula—but in the wake of losing Helen, I'm beginning to see that she's a true warrior for women. She might sit on the side of the law that deemed each of us "guilty," but she actually sees the humanity in each of us. Superintendent Lord holds high standards for our behavior because she believes we can improve ourselves and our lives, and in a very personal way, she wants us to grow.

After watching how I cared for Helen, it seems that Superintendent Lord has begun to see me with new eyes.

Or maybe, like me, she is beginning to see a different Donna.

The ACE program is well received at the prison, and over time, more and more women seek out our support services. Perhaps the most significant development occurs when Superintendent Lord allows for a hospice unit to be set up in the prison. Our group of women receives training to provide hospice care to our sisters who are now journeying through the stages of death. The role of those of us in the ACE program is to make them feel more comfortable—we rub cream on their feet, we freshen their mouths with a sip of water or ginger ale, we gently apply ointment to their dry lips and call for medical help whenever they're in pain.

Also, if they want us to, we pray with them. Women of so many different backgrounds, ethnicities, and religions inhabit this prison, but especially among the dying, all we need to share is a collective faith in something greater than us. One of the most powerful insights of my life is what a blessing it is to be at someone's side as they're preparing to exit this life. I'll never forget what it was like to hold Adrienne as she took her first breaths and met the world with wide eyes. Getting to witness the completion of the cycle of life makes me feel as though I've been chosen among a blessed few as we stand by the prison chaplain, Rev. Maria Lopez, when she anoints the dying woman and offers a prayer for her peace and comfort.

Within a year of ACE's launch, I earn certification to be an HIV counselor and am placed on regular work detail in the prison coordinating HIV discussion groups, setting up counseling for grieving women in the process of losing a dear friend, and training caregivers. I earn an hourly wage of twenty-five cents, which is enough to buy stamps to write letters to Adrienne, Dalida, and some of my friends outside, and to buy treats like ice cream, potato chips, peanut butter, and jelly. The small, everyday items I can purchase from the commissary are a luxury, but far more satisfying than these is the emergence of this new sense of self. Every single day I arrive for my shift, I'm astonished that I can help others in this way. I'm gaining clarity that my heart and mind contain a positive purpose. When I lie in my cell at night, it brings tears to my eyes to think of how my work makes me feel. I am so much more than a body for other people to treat in any way they want. For the first time, someone needs and appreciates me.

I feel worthy.

For women who are infected with HIV and for so many of us others, this groundbreaking AIDS program is transformative inside the prison. However, on a state level, there are challenges brewing. As the ACE program becomes established and begins to grow, state politicians in Albany question Superintendent Lord on whether the program is the most effective way for state money to be spent at the prison. Each time she makes the trip to fight on our behalf, she provides us with updates. There's an increasing appreciation throughout the prison that the superintendent isn't just here to punish us. She's on our side, and she refuses to give up. "You're women," she tells our central group of change-makers. "Who else could tell us what you need?"

Her will and the progress we're all making together motivates a core group of us to create more programs at Bedford that will support the wellness and self-esteem of individuals here and empower the most marginalized among us. A dozen of us band together and dub ourselves "the Agents of Change," and true to their style, Judy and Kathy pick a folksy, hippie song to serve as our anthem. Together, we sing "Sister" by Cris Williamson:

Believe on me, I am your friend…
I will fold you in my arms like a white-winged dove…

My life is officially no longer about survival or doing what I have to do just to get by. As one of these women, I'm now part of something larger, something more important. *You're different than the others.* There's not a day I don't hear Mr. V's words in my head. However, my goodness and my courage no longer leave me alone on my own island. Now I'm part of a shared mission to make this place better.

When Helen died, I said farewell not only to her but also to who I was before I knew her. I no longer need to stand by, to stay silent when something bad happens to me or to another woman. From this point, I'm my own person, focusing wholly on my goodness and my growth.

7

MOTHER MARY AND THE END OF VIOLENCE

As Superintendent Lord continues to affirm our efforts by standing up for us in Albany, I pay more attention to the discussions and decisions that happen in the state capitol and how they affect us as incarcerated women.

I learn that in 1985, one year before I arrived at Bedford, something happened in the State of New York that had never happened before: hearings took place in Albany in which incarcerated women from prisons around the state spoke before legislators to share their very personal stories about how they wound up in prison. In many cases, they were convicted for killing their abusers.

Following those hearings, Governor Mario Cuomo created the Governor's Commission on Domestic Violence and appointed a woman named Charlotte Watson as its director. Some directors

at Bedford then organized an internal program, working in col-
laboration with the governor's special department to address the
very real problems that are happening in the lives of women here at
Bedford and even throughout New York State.

As I deepen my engagement with the Agents of Change, Sharon Smolick, who's the director of this internal family violence
program at Bedford, calls for me to visit her office. I approach and
knock on her door unsurely, noting concern on her face as she
invites me to take a seat. "I know about your crime, Donna," she
says.

In an instant, my face flushes hot with shame. *I've been working to overcome all that, and the prison administrators see it. Why is
she bringing this up right now?*

"And I know that you've faced a lot of struggle in your life."

I look up at her, still not sure where this conversation is headed.
"How do you know that?" There are times when I hear that my
voice is still shrouded in defensiveness.

"Because," she tells me. "Pain recognizes pain." Sharon goes
on to reveal to me that she did time at a prison in Florida because
of hurt and brokenness in her own past. She asks me to open up
about my upbringing, and I feel myself relax. A trust and closeness
with Sharon begins to emerge, as she says she's seen how involved
I've become with causes around here. Then she does the truly
unexpected when she asks me, "Donna, would you like to participate in our Domestic Family Violence Program?"

I've heard about this program, which is the first of its kind in
the nation. Sharon runs it with a popular figure around the prison:

Sr. Mary Nerney, a nun and psychologist who volunteers her expertise to the group a few times each month. Sr. Mary was a key player in the 1985 women's hearings in Albany which successfully resulted in the creation of the governor's department for domestic violence. Since the 1970s, Sr. Mary has gone before political decision-makers to demonstrate how there are often personal narratives of having been battered among incarcerated women. Her argument is that in many cases, that violent past directly or indirectly led to the crimes for which a woman has been convicted.

With honor, I accept Sharon's invitation to join the group and find that this group setting is a chance to gain a kind of perspective on my own past that will permanently change me. I have always felt so alone *in* my abuse, and *because* of my abuse. But here in the Domestic Family Violence Program, every single woman around me has suffered violence at the hands of a boyfriend or husband, a father or mother, a grandparent or stepparent, an uncle, a teacher, or others. As we share around the room, each story is as unfortunate as the one before it. Our turmoils are varied but vivid, and each of us is a woman who has had to resort to extreme circumstances to try to save her own life. One seventeen-year-old, whom we all know as Love, was abused by her mother, just like me and like several of us...but when Love was just eleven years old, her mother did something far worse: she introduced her daughter to heroin.

Needing love and approval and not knowing healthy guidance, Love became hooked on the drug. Hand in hand with her drug use came a need for money to buy it, and hand in hand with that came sexual violence. Young Love became involved with an older man, a thief who used her as bait in his robberies. That's what led to her getting caught.

I begin to open up and share about my story, but as I listen to the stories of the other women, their pain becomes my pain. There are some women who experienced sexual abuse from the age of two, some from the age of five. I can see myself in their stories, and I can understand how they arrived here—not only in prison, but at such low points in their lives.

Back in my cell following that first meeting, I weep as I think more about Love's story. So much of it was relatable for me: the abusive parent, the older man who promises a route to escape. There's something about motherhood that softens the heart and helps a woman to see her child in every child she meets. There's an innocence in Love's face that reminds me of my daughter and makes it impossible for me to imagine how her mother could have done what she did. I stop myself just short of judging this woman I've never met, as I'm beginning to understand how abuse shapes our choices, as well as our perceptions of what it is to love and be loved.

As we go around the room, meeting after meeting, the reality is searing: every single woman among us has experienced abuse at some point in her life. The more stories I hear, the sicker I feel. *This is wrong!*

This is wrong.

For the first time, I stop asking, *Why am I the only one?*

Instead, I ask: *Why am I NOT the only one?*

The fact is undeniable: there's a link between rates of brutal domestic violence and a prison full of wounded, broken, silenced, crying, desperate women. It's also infuriating to learn that not a single one of us was allowed to share our personal histories in court to reveal how the series of brutal events in our lives might have led to our crimes.

Soon I'm so entrenched in the Family Domestic Violence program that I become one of its principal organizers. With the support of Superintendent Lord, and under the guidance of Sharon Smolick, a group of us works further to break out different categories of abuse and develop therapeutic groups for the women who have experienced each one. We establish a group for victims of sexual abuse, one for victims of incest, and one for victims of ritual abuse. There's a place for victims of domestic violence, and even groups for women who have killed their child or their batterer, as well as a group for women who are pedophiles. We treat every single one of them as human—how else can they change? We want to offer a space for understanding to all of these women, and we want prison life to be honest and authentic.

We also hold larger group sessions, where everyone from the various groups comes together to share, explore, discuss…and perhaps even find solutions for ourselves or for women outside who may be at risk. No matter what each of us has done or experienced, our stories reveal the truth: there's a pattern. For every female behind bars, there is a girl outside who will share the same future unless someone takes action *now* to help her.

The governor's office works with us to hold a follow-up hearing to their conversations on domestic violence in Albany at Bedford. I volunteer to help set up the prison gymnasium for the hearing. This small act of service becomes the most pivotal moment in my entire life experience when I begin to grow personally familiar with Sr. Mary Nerney.

Everyone who knows her loves this broad Irish woman with a smile as big as her heart. As we prepare for the hearing, I walk alongside to assist her while she hangs T-shirts around the gym that feature phrases or stories from us women that represent our abuse or our hope for a better life. She uses bobby pins to link all the T-shirts together, symbolic of the way we women have bonded to create a bigger, better reality for ourselves and each other here in prison.

In this one-on-one exchange in the gymnasium, Sr. Mary begins to very gently invite me to open up about myself. Maybe it's because of the way she takes charge and inspires all of us to cooperate so smoothly, or maybe it's because she shows interest in me personally... but there's something about Sr. Mary that I take to very naturally.

I expand a little on the stories I've shared in our Domestic Family Violence group, and I begin to ask her about her background, too. She reveals she's from the Sisters of Notre Dame order of Catholic nuns, and she and her sisters minister specifically to women. Just as I've been experiencing in not getting to see Adrienne, Sr. Mary knows there's usually more than one victim to every crime. "When you sentence a woman to jail," she says, "you sentence the whole family."

I pay close attention when Sr. Mary is formally introduced at the hearing in our gymnasium. She's made a profound impact on many women, having founded STEPS to End Family Violence, a program that provides legal assistance and psychological counseling to battered women (including those imprisoned for killing their abusers), as well as battered men and other family members who witness domestic violence. In 1975, Sr. Mary also founded Greenhope Services for Women, which helps to reintegrate incarcerated women into society and teaches them the construction trades, and the Incarcerated Mothers Program, which keeps the children of inmates out of the foster care system by placing them with family members. I grasp onto this information about Sr. Mary, finding further hope and comfort about the fact she's done work with incarcerated women and their children.

From this point, Sr. Mary and I begin to grow closer. She turns to us women to brainstorm how to go about creating bills, awareness, and movements to get battered women out of prisons. "What can we do?" she asks us. We share our ideas with her, and she fights until the governor releases one battered woman from prison.

This shows me the need to get the legislation in place for this issue, and she and I discuss a bill she's creating to give people a chance to get out of prison on good time if they prove that domestic violence was a significant factor throughout their lives that led to their crime. I don't even know it yet, but Sr. Mary is beginning to involve me politically, as an activist.

With her at the helm, I become part of a group that creates a committee on the inside known as the Violence Against Women

Committee. Sr. Mary uses our committee as a sounding board and a model for the work she's doing on the outside. *Inside-out, inside-out*: this is our model. The work we do and the conversations we have here inside begin to influence and transform what's happening outside—in government, in other prisons, and in other women's lives outside of Bedford. This work has become my purpose in life, my passion...my *thing*. I begin to wonder whether there was a reason, a larger plan, behind why I experienced those impossibly painful first twenty-one years of my life. Inspiring and supporting women who need it has become my calling. It's the reason I exist.

One day, Sr. Mary enters the prison holding a bag filled up with candy—her trademark. The security guards at the prison entrance always tease her at the routine bag check station. "Really, Sister?" they ask her. "You're going to eat all these sweets today?"

"This is my lunch," she tells them. They laugh, knowing she loves to bring us women candy every time she's here.

Her spirit makes me giggle. "Nuns aren't supposed to lie," I tell her. "Not even about candy."

"Well," she scoffs playfully. "I'm sure I can be forgiven this, don't you think?"

That is her love. So human, and at the same time, so transcendent and divine.

Sr. Mary is so thoughtful that to help us save the money we spend at the commissary, she brings greeting cards for us to send out to our loved ones for their birthdays, and cards that say *thinking of you*, or *thank you*. She updates us on the news in the world, what the conversation is in Albany, and the movements that are taking place. One day, as she's speaking to me, I respond to her: "Thanks for filling me in, Mother." Since I met her, I've contemplated doing this. When it comes out of my mouth, it's the most natural thing in the world.

She looks at me. I look at her.

She looks at me. "Oh, stop," she says, pretending to wave me away with her hand.

"Why, Mother?"

"Shh!" she laughs, looking at the guards standing nearby. "Don't let anyone hear you say that!"

"Ain't nobody gonna pay us any mind... Mother."

She hides a coy smile until we both begin to laugh. In our friendship and our partnership until now, it has been as though something spiritual has indeed been gestating. Now, suddenly, our relationship solidifies. We don't get to choose our birth mothers, nor did I choose my adoptive mother... but on this day with this one word, I've chosen the woman who will be my mother for the rest of my life. To me, Sr. Mary—Mother—is like a modern-day Joan of Arc: strong and fierce with passion for what she believes in. I'll never forget how I was struck the first moment I saw her: she had skin so pure white it seemed almost translucent, a halo of short white hair, and the face of an angel. She stood tall and broad-shouldered, as though she was prepared to bear any burden. And she had a regal aura. My heart and spirit fell in love with her right away, as if I were her daughter and she were my rightful mother.

After this, she no longer debates with me when I refer to her by the most intimate title I've ever called anyone: *Mother.* We begin to grow so close that at one point, she finally tells me: "Just call me Mom." That word never felt so happy or so true on my lips.

It so happens that it's also the word that stirs a feeling of uneasiness inside me and reminds me of my greatest shortcoming. In spite of the strides and discoveries I've made in my life in the past few years, there's one particular area in which I still ache for help. When my daughter is thirteen years old, it has been over five years since I last saw her during that fleeting hearing in family court. From the day she was born and even before that, when I carried Adrienne inside me, I vowed to her that we'd be bonded for life and that I would always be there to take care of her. Prison has shown me that in the majority of cases, we women have wound up here because the love in our lives has been deficient, defective, or deprived. Our relationships with our children are an opportunity for us to replenish the love that's bled out of us in our traumas, not to mention the chance to make society a better place by raising and influencing our children with the insight we've gained. I've experienced very personally what it is not to have deeply loving guidance—how can our society expect us to succeed as parents when we can't see our children? How can we even hope for the cycle of violence and bad choices to be broken when we have no influence? After more than five years inside prison, I've pursued trainings, earned certifications, and even made a little money with my job as an HIV counselor. I have friends—family—and a mission that we share. Ever so steadily, these pieces of my life have moved into place, just like a puzzle, and begun to make me whole. But there's one aspect of my life, of my crime, that will never allow my life to be whole: no matter what I do to cultivate peace and growth, I cannot accept life without Adrienne. She's almost a teenager now. Even if she weren't preparing to enter the stage in her life that for me led to dangerous decisions from which I could never turn back, I can only ever be content *with myself* when I know I'm a part of her life.

In 1992, I share this with Sr. Mary and her colleague, Sr. Elaine Roulet, who accompanied me to family court on that day five years ago. More and more, Sr. Elaine's programs for families of the incarcerated are becoming models for many prisons around the country. Now I need her and Sr. Mary to provide me with wisdom that will become the model for my life.

With Sr. Mary behind me, Sr. Elaine and I begin to develop a strategy for her to work with the court and set up a real visit with my little girl. In turn, Sr. Elaine partners closely with my attorney to make it clear to the court that Bedford has a proven program for children visiting their mothers. The visits will be supervised, she states, and Sr. Elaine and her colleagues will even provide us with lunch. Then she drives the point home that I'm not in prison for any crime that was child-related. *Did you tell them I love my child?* More than five years ago when I was arrested, my adoptive father dismissed his single opportunity to help me succeed in my most important role, as a mother, by refusing to vouch for my parenting. This folly and so many committed by others have stacked the odds against us. But Sr. Elaine returns from court with a lightness in her face: the court has granted me the right to see Adrienne.

Alone in the visitation room, I don't look at the clock. The minutes before her arrival creep slowly, and I know the hours together will fly. Memories of Adrienne's childhood begin to light up in my mind, how the neighbor ladies in Harlem would insist on handing me money to buy her toys at the drugstore and ruffled little dresses. I remember a time on the train during the holiday season shortly before the crime happened. I worked a lot and lived downstairs with Rita and Theresa, but I remember how I mothered Adrienne with every chance I got. I never felt as fulfilled as I did when it was just the two of us against the world. I remember I was wearing my old blue puffy winter coat, and Adrienne, then just a toddler, sat next to me on the subway. I was watching the city go by through the subway window, and when I looked down at her, she was staring up at me with her big brown eyes. In that moment was the seal of permanent love. I've referenced that exchange on occasion in my mind. It was as if, in some way, we both knew that something was coming that would threaten to tear us apart and that we were locking the love of this moment to live inside our hearts forever.

Then she walks through the door. Alvin slowly enters behind her. I race to my little girl, wrap my arms around her shoulders, and breathe deeply; she's carried in the scent of fresh air. When I release her from my embrace and stand her back for a good look, I can't help but study everything about her: the innocence in her posture, the pure honesty in her eyes, the unassuming way she tucks her hands inside her pockets. Three words I've wanted to say for five years swell inside me until I can no longer keep them from crossing my lips: "I love you!" She has a way of dropping her gaze that suggests she feels ashamed, confused... torn.

Alvin waits silently at the edge of the visitation room for a full six hours while Adrienne and I spend time nearby in the Children's Center playroom. I use the activities as a way to ease into conversation, though her answers to my questions are brief and her glances toward me are tentative... but in the brief flash of a second, she tells me with her eyes that she's yearning for something— more time together, more affection, more of *me*?

From conception, a mother is supposed to be able to feed her little one, and a deep gratitude fills me when the nuns deliver lunch to us on trays. There's a politeness between us as Adrienne and I eat together, slowly and carefully—despite how hungry our souls are. For this one afternoon, I will be totally nourished. I can only pray that this time together will sustain Adrienne, too.

When it's time for her to leave, again I take Adrienne in my arms. I glance only for a split second at Alvin, who's glaring over my daughter's shoulder. With our cheeks pressed together, a hint of my little girl's voice comes muffled through my ear, which at first I think is from a gentle effort to push me away... until I realize that she's crying. I squeeze a little tighter, and tell her once more: "I love you."

In my ear, so that Alvin can't hear her, she whispers sweetly: "Bye-bye, Mommy."

With this, I know I have to let go. Judy Clark's words chime in my head as I watch Adrienne walk to her father: the inevitable goodbye makes each preceding minute of the visit so sorely difficult.

But now I have something to hold on to. My mother has helped me to mother. She and her sister in faith have helped me show my daughter that my love for her is real. I've seen her. I've held her. I've smelled her scent and touched her skin.

And my little girl just called me Mommy.

8

AN EDUCATION

Affirming my life in such a way that they would help make a reality of my need to see my child, women like Sr. Mary and the rest of my Jail Sisters have made me believe for the first time that I can succeed at the dreams that have been most important to me. When the door closes on a wish we hold for our future, a light in our soul is snuffed out. But I'm beginning to see that our lives don't have to end when we come to prison. It takes a fierce optimism and unshaking commitment, but even while we're inside, we *can* in fact grow into the best we can be.

Superintendent Lord, Kathy, Judy, and a few other women recently have gotten a grassroots school initiative going to bring fully accredited college degree programs and professors to the prison through Mercy College, a formal higher education institution. Almost twenty years have passed since my days as "the

Golden Child" who was destined for an Ivy League education, but now I do something I thought I might miss out on forever: I enroll to work toward a bachelor's degree in behavioral sciences with a concentration in social psychology.

Our "campus" is surrounded by barbed wire and armed prison guards—but when the classroom doors shut and I look up at our professor working on the blackboard, I'm no longer in prison. I'm like the hummingbirds I remember from my childhood, drinking in the juice of life—

In the classroom, I'm free.

When I was a little girl reading *Dibs in Search of Self*, I dreamed about the possibility of one day earning a doctorate degree and becoming an academic just like my adoptive mother. (I know that was her dream for me, too.) I try to think back to the moment when my life changed so pivotally that I gave up on that dream... then it hits me: it was when Alvin took me away.

But now I can feel possibility tapping on my shoulder ever so gently. I grab ahold of it, and I absorb every idea our professors share with us. I begin to spend my free minutes in quiet study or reading textbooks and some classic works of fiction whose names I remember from when I was a child.

Like my soul mother, Sr. Mary, I want to understand why women like me end up convicted criminals and what we can do to prevent it from happening to other women. My confidence and self-awareness grow as I find myself able to engage with Sr. Mary in conversations about her work as a professional in psychology, spirituality, and human behavior. I write essays and take quizzes and exams, but the astonishment of my new reality never wanes: after all the awards and accolades I'd earned in school as a teen-ager, my first-rate education has turned out to be at a maximum-security prison.

In my psychology classes, my mind opens in a way that helps me deepen some of my prison relationships in a healthy way... and to be discerning about some others. In the early 1990s, a group of women has recently arrived to my unit at Bedford that includes Carolyn Warmus and Pamela Smart, who live in the "high profile" unit. Carolyn is a Detroit heiress and schoolteacher sentenced to twenty-five years to life for the 1989 murder of her lover's wife, which was a crime that drew national attention for its similarity to the film *Fatal Attraction*. Pam is a former high school media coordinator from New Hampshire convicted of conspiring with her fifteen-year-old lover and his friends to kill her husband. She's serving a sentence of life in prison without the chance of parole.

Carolyn is usually cool and elusive with random spurts of emo-tion. When anyone brings up the murder of her ex-lover's wife, she denies that she was the one who did it. Pam Smart is just the opposite. She grows tearful when she speaks of her husband and the pain she carries for having gotten involved with her teen lover. Even here, her love knows no bounds, but in the best way. Pam is a woman of great intellect and emotional intelligence, and she gives her time to others when they need legal insight, or some help studying.

Our unit is quite the motley crew of backgrounds and tem-peraments, especially when we congregate together in the unit's small kitchen. Anyone who's been here for any amount of time knows to be suspicious of the prison's mess hall, so with coolers and hot plates, we each set out and forage for provisions to improvise our own meals: a can of tuna, some seasoning from the commissary, mayonnaise from someone's family care package. With some bread we sneak out of the mess hall, and we do what women do when circumstances throw us together: we talk, argue, prepare food, sit down together, and share meals.

And we open up—about our children, our studies, our futures... and about the crimes of which we've been convicted. Kathy and Judy begin to challenge me in a way that sets me on edge when they both suggest I might want to go about my participation in the college program in a more mature way. I'm one of the youngest in the program, and apparently, even though I'm intelligent, I've been acting young. At this, I feel like they're teaming up against me, and instantly I'm transported back in time to my childhood when Daphne told me that I wasn't quite as bright as the other children I'd meet at boarding school. "Who the fuck do you think you are?" I ask the two of them one day. *Nobody gets to tell me how and who I should be!*

I'm fuming, ready to turn to other women to take my side, until I remember that I have a resource I've never had before: Mother. She invites me to think their intentions through, to reflect, to pray that in time I'll be able to have enough perspective to see their point. I listen to Mother humbly, knowing there are parts of me that are still very hurt and broken.

Back in our unit, I ask myself whether I can see Judy and Kathy through the lens of knowing the positive change they're trying to make in a war-torn country and world. That's when it dawns on me that Judy and Kathy are speaking from their place of seeing potential in me.

I open up to this group of women about the remorse that I continue to carry about not helping Mr. V when I had the chance. I'm not sure I'll ever know how to forgive myself for that, or for the fact that I still harbor anger toward people in my past. I feel empathy for the women who surround me, knowing that for many of us, it was circumstances in our lives that have brought us here.

Periodically there are peers going before us who carry a torch and light the way for us to try and follow. Jean Harris is an incarcerated woman at Bedford who has played an instrumental role for many women inside. She's a natural leader for women and children as the former longtime headmistress of a prominent school for girls outside of Washington, D.C., before her 1981 conviction for killing her love interest—a case that made national headlines due in part to her professional position and also to the fact that her lover was Herman Tarnower, a cardiologist who had authored the best-selling 1970s diet book, *The Complete Scarsdale Medical Diet*. Jean is polished and poised, and some women at Bedford have claimed she has an upper-class air about her... but with her intellect, perseverance, and openness to share herself, she inspires me.

During Jean's time in prison, she has established an academically rigorous scholarship program for the children of incarcerated women. This program enables some of the brightest of these kids to attend prestigious boarding schools, encouraging them to optimize their opportunities to be educated well. This route is a far better option than falling between the cracks in their public schools, their communities, and in society with the prospect of getting involved in crimes themselves.

Jean Harris has also assisted Sr. Elaine in teaching a parenting class to inmates, as well as a nursery program for women who entered prison while they were pregnant.

By 1992, she has served twelve years of a fifteen-year-to-life sentence. The women band around Jean as she fights in her fourth bout for clemency—a decision from the court that a sentence has been sufficiently served with no remaining requirements. Anytime this is a possibility for one of the women here, a feeling of possibility elevates the hope of the entire prison. Clemency is an idea that I can't yet imagine for myself. I still carry too much guilt and shame, feeling as though I don't deserve compassion. But oh, how I want it for my sisters.

Jean's fight is emotional for all of us. In the midst of it, she suffers a heart attack: the third time this has happened to her in prison. It's always been obvious that Jean regrets what she did, and the crime has taken a toll on her in every way. Many women at Bedford hope and pray fervently for her to heal and get out before her sentence is up. In 1993, two years earlier than her minimum sentence, Jean Harris is released from prison.

For me, this is the first small ray of light shining potential onto what I have feared would be impossible in my case. Now, I see: maybe we "lifers" really will have a chance to live to see our children succeed from the outside. Jean's legacy is powerful. For me personally, she's proven that even while we're here, there's hope for the futures of incarcerated women *and* our children.

A few correctional officers react to Jean's parole with open scoffs, calling it typical white privilege. But for us women, she has made important progress. We embrace Jean Harris's departure as a symbol that there is in fact increasing humanity in our society. How can we change the present and the future without proof that humanity exists?

9

DAUGHTERS AND A CIRCLE OF ABUSE

On a sunny June afternoon in 1994, my life has begun to surge with the feeling that possibility abounds when I don a second-hand, donated cap and gown and celebrate my graduation inside the prison's gym. In pride, I grip my diploma—a bachelor of science in the behavioral sciences. I've always wanted an advanced education, but for so long I was afraid I'd messed it up by running away from home at age fourteen. Unlike some of the other women, I don't have family there to celebrate with me. Seeing Adrienne in the audience would be, as I like to say, the candle on the icing on the cake.

But that summer, Sr. Elaine provides me with something even better. Thanks to the ways women like her and Jean Harris have pushed for us to be able to care for our children from inside, Adrienne is invited to spend the summer at the home of a local family in the town of Bedford, making it possible for my daughter and me to see each other every day. This time, Alvin can do nothing about it: for the first time since I arrived at prison, the judge has decided that this arrangement will be beneficial to Adrienne and is simply part of my rights as her mother.

The kindness of her host family further softens my heart as Adrienne reports how friendly they are. They've taken her on a couple of family outings, they take care of her meals, they buy her books and face paints that she brings to the prison for us to have fun with together. As she begins to visit me daily, a side of my daughter emerges that I haven't gotten to witness since she was a baby: no longer between us are there downcast eyes, sadness, and a sense of estrangement. Instead, she comes to me smiling, gradually more comfortable. The prison staff welcomes her, the nuns provide us with lunch and cakes, and most days, my daughter and I have hours of uninterrupted time together. We stay entertained putting makeup on each other and making snacks, like microwaveable mini-burgers and pizzas, with the makeshift ingredients we can find from the prison vending machines, like cheese sticks and smoked sausage.

Adrienne tells me about her friends at school, her interests, her favorite subjects, how her grandmother Dorothy encourages her learning and achievement. I begin to see how my little girl has a mind for science and technology (Dorothy has even bought her a microscope), as well as an unfiltered honesty that comes with a kind of courage that I'm only learning to cultivate now, as an adult. Adrienne's strength and focus in the face of what she's lived through, without having me as her mother constantly present, stun me.

Together we participate in the talent show the prison puts on, dressing up in costume. As we sing and dance for the audience that claps and cheers us on, I can sense we both feel free from the everyday worries of both our lives. Every day we're together, Adrienne makes me laugh, as her silly side emerges more and more. She is my light. From the time she arrived early in the summer, it takes very little time for her to melt from the coldness of Alvin's oversight. She tells me, "Thank you, Mommy," and "Yes, please, Mommy." My child is kind and gentle-spirited, and seems to accept my doting on her with pleasure.

In very private moments, Adrienne opens up to share with me what goes on inside Alvin's home. My insides clench at the disturbance of it and my heart sears with hurt. His tendencies toward physical and emotional abuse play out differently to Adrienne than they did toward me, but they are just as mean and damaging.

Alvin has married a woman whom he demands that Adrienne call Mommy. "But I won't do it," Adrienne says, with her arms crossed.

"Why's that?"

She looks at me with sincerity in her eyes. "Because I already have a mother."

I have to keep a strong expression on my face to avoid weeping in appreciation of her loyalty to me.

She tells me about her half siblings now that Alvin's had more children, and how her father and stepmother sometimes force Adrienne to sit in the corner of the kitchen with no plate in front of her while the rest of the family passes dishes of food right past her. I make note of all these offenses to share with Sr. Elaine, though by now I'm tragically aware of how limited my influence is on what happens when Adrienne is not with me.

When September arrives and it's time for her to return to the city, neither of us can hide our tears. It's a twisted combination of distress for Adrienne's safety with the reality that we'll be separated for an amount of time we can't predict. We've grown so close this summer; for the first time, we're both certain of how much each loves the other. Now, it's likely Alvin will make Adrienne pay a price for what should be the safest, most natural thing in the world: this love between a mother and daughter.

With my degree in hand and a summer with my daughter, this has been the brightest time I've known in years, but indeed the darkness sets in swiftly again and complicates life in many ways. In September 1994, President Clinton signs the Violent Crime Control and Law Enforcement Act, known more commonly as "the Crime Bill," whose main pillars are to offer billions of dollars of increased funding for the operation of prisons, to increase the number of law enforcement officers nationally, and fund programs for the prevention of violent crime. To the public, it all sounds very utopian, but there's a lesser-known aspect of the bill that makes it an unfortunate event for many women I know here: inmates are no longer permitted to receive government funding through the Pell Grant to pursue a higher education while they're in prison.

I am one of the very fortunate ones, as I've just recently graduated. However, there are many women at Bedford who have just started to pursue their education, or, even worse, they're just a few credits away from attaining their degrees. I know how so many of them must feel: that the one chance they've been given in life has just been ripped away. Many of us are women, working for a chance in life—but it feels like in the eyes of the rest of the world, we're nothing.

The response at Bedford is one of hopelessness, the feeling that the education program gave us a chance to be better, but now there's nothing for us to work toward. Learning fills the mind with understanding, new awakenings, and awareness about the self, the environment, and the world an individual lives in. To someone hearing about this controversy on the news, it might sound as though an inmate in a prison shouldn't have a right to a higher education, or even need an education. But President Clinton's signing of the Crime Bill calls attention to the fact that as a society, we need to understand justice much differently: very often, when a crime is committed, it's because a marginalized person is really just looking for an opportunity to improve his or her life. The problem in our country is that black people, brown people, many Asians, and poor white people typically don't find access to something better in life, or readily available contacts to mentor them, guide them, or help them make valuable connections or even productive decisions. My situation is a case in point, and my studies toward my bachelor degree taught me a great deal about how I was affected growing up and the behavior patterns and reactions that led to my involvement with the crime that ultimately ended Mr. V's life.

The Crime Bill is a huge source of discouragement for those of us inside—especially those of us who are in fact rehabilitating, working to improve ourselves and learning to gain some perspective on why a crime might have taken place and what our role was in it. An education, a chance to learn and improve ourselves, is critical. Ninety-seven percent of incarcerated people return home. Doesn't society want them to transition back to the world as better people than they were before they were incarcerated?

Inside prison, I'm one of a group of women who decide to take education into our own hands. While there were four hundred women at Bedford when I arrived here, in the past decade the number has doubled. In many cases the new inmates are very young women, even teens. I develop a curriculum to help build responsibility, coping skills, and self-esteem among sixteen- to twenty-five-year-olds. The program is designed to give them what I never had: a voice and a safe space to grow and learn and overcome difficult childhoods. Again, at a rate of twenty-five cents per hour, I love helping these young women accomplish this goal and feel hope for a better future—somehow, somewhere. Helping them to identify and draw out their strengths also deepens my own inner healing, as though I'm nurturing the troubled teen who still lives inside of me.

After this program is fully established, Pamela Smart becomes instrumentally involved. She and I both work to help other women get their high school equivalency certificates and prepare them to go on to college. Pam's patience for the women never fails to touch me. She has the heart for helping other women, and because of her personal strength, she's uniquely able to reemphasize and reinforce their intelligence and potential. They behold her so thankfully, and it's visibly possible to witness many of them realizing for the first time: *Oh my God. I am smart. My mind is actually worth something.* When you've been told as far back as childhood that you're worthless, you're stupid, or nobody ever wanted you, there will come a point when you start to believe it. But an individual's self-perception can change when someone tells them for the first time: *You're better than that. You're not who they've said you are.* Many times, we see women begin to form an identity of their own—one that's positive. Helping these women accomplish their academic goals makes me believe in a better future. Their hope is my hope, and my hope is theirs. We're sisters.

These triumphs bring us together and affect many women at Bedford powerfully... until a trauma strikes for the most important young woman in my life that will cause me to tumble down into an intense, pained isolation.

In August 1995, a year after the summer she spent with me, I receive a call with news that rocks me: Adrienne has gone missing from her father's house. She's now fourteen years old, the very same age I was when I could no longer endure the rapes I experienced routinely inside Roy and Daphne's home. My daughter has lived through a great deal of pain, but I fear that only the worst would make her run away. I call around to a few friends who go out on a search. This time, no one is able to find her.

I'm sick, sleepless, panicked for days. Finally, within a week, Adrienne shows up at the only place she knew she would feel safe: here at Bedford. Together we sit in the visiting room, and I know in my gut what she's about to tell me. Her face drops. "Mommy," she says quietly, "you're the only one who will believe me..."

No. Please, not this.

Adrienne goes on to tell me that the boyfriend of one of Alvin's sisters has raped her. Her words knock the air out of me—and then, it gets worse: she describes it happening many times.

Since my childhood, I've become an expert at detaching from my own pain—but hearing about my daughter's pain causes me to double over, trying to fully catch my breath as my mind spins with chaos and my heart goes sick. I can't see clearly through the emotions I feel, but as I get my fingers around an iota of composure, one thing is certain: I'm going to do what my mother never did. I calm myself long enough to move in and put my arms around my daughter. "I believe you," I tell her, and as I hold her, both of us cry together. "I promise you," I tell her. "You are not going back to that house!"

She wipes her eyes with her fists and locks her gaze in mine. "You really promise?" she says.

And I do. When she was born, I promised that I would protect her, and now is the time to fight. I don't want Adrienne's life to follow the way mine went. It's taken me almost thirty-one years to begin to overcome the life I was born with. I have to stop the cycle of violence against women and girls. The futures of our daughters depend on this.

I usually turn to women in the prison for support and advice in times like this, but for Adrienne's sake, I want to keep the situation private. In the days to follow, I work closely with Superintendent Lord and Sharon Smolick to call the child abuse hotline and child protective services to file a report and arrange medical attention for Adrienne through the court. A team of healthcare professionals runs some testing, and a doctor diagnoses Adrienne with a venereal disease that could render her unable to have children in the future. Whether she wants to have children or not, I am momentarily paralyzed in my distress. My daughter's health, safety, and well-being have been totally compromised, and her innocence—that little light inside her heart—has been stolen.

I arrange for protective custody for Adrienne and pursue criminal charges against the perpetrator. I stay strong for my daughter, being her voice and her advocate, and most importantly, making sure she knows that she did nothing wrong. I speak out for her. I make noise. I want her to know that she doesn't have to be silent when anyone hurts her, even if—*especially* if—it's a relative. Being family doesn't mean we're obligated to keep it a secret when someone takes advantage of us.

I feel like I'm fighting on behalf of us both, decades of fury radiating from my core. I've heard that anger is a powerful stimulus toward change, but shortly, in its place begin to spill those longer practiced and far less empowering feelings: guilt, pain…shame. The truth of this is that I feel like the one who deserves blame for my daughter's rape. I wasn't there, and I allowed it to happen.

The nightmares begin again. It's Selma, looking down at me

through the window of my cell, trying to get to me. It's Alvin, urinating on me in the corner of a bare apartment. It's Roy, and the smell of moth balls combined with shoe leather and Daphne's perfume inside that dark closet.

It's Mr. V:

Will you help me?

I often wake to the sound of my own cry: *HELP HIM!*

My incapacity to help, over and over, has ruined lives. I curl up and think of my daughter, tears soaking my pillow until it's time to rise and report to breakfast.

And in a way I couldn't have anticipated, I'll serve time for the way I've failed Adrienne. Trying to be a voice for her vulnerability is about to put me in a position that creates yet another prison that, in some ways, is more complex than anything I've experienced yet.

10

FINDING OUR VOICES

Adrienne is placed in a psychiatric hospital to deal with the emotional difficulties that have built up throughout the course of her life and come to a head with this routine sexual assault. I pray that my little girl is safe, and that this will be a chance for her to heal... though I know very well that rape is a prison that comes with a life sentence of inner conflict—a lesson that I'm about to learn yet another time too many.

Up to now, prison has been the first place in my life where I'm safe from day-to-day abuse and protected by authority figures in my life who care. When I learn what Adrienne has experienced, I report it to the administrators at the prison and inform them that I intend to pursue criminal charges. Because they know how passionate I am about the programs I'm involved in for women, they're supportive of the fight that I'll face as I work to ensure that Adrienne's rapist sees consequences for what he's done to my child. Superintendent Lord assures me that she and her colleagues will accommodate my phone calls and court appearances when the case against him gets under way.

To facilitate this, she puts an officer who I will call CO Brown in charge of my case. CO Brown is known around the prison as a volatile, intimidating brute of a man. He gets respect, but it's not genuine—it's only due to the fear he instills in us women. He wouldn't be the first choice for my go-to whenever I need to return a phone call about Adrienne's incident, but I have to take the support that Superintendent Lord has offered to me.

Even in the moments when I'm not dealing with Adrienne's case, CO Brown begins to follow me around the prison as though he's growing fixated on me. Soon, he begins to corner me in isolated areas and force himself on me. He says that if I report this, he won't permit me to communicate with all the necessary parties for Adrienne's case. If I won't do what he wants, my daughter won't get the help she needs—the worst possible way anyone could hurt me right now.

I'm already heartbroken as I'm trying to save my little girl from the hell she's been living without me, but being cornered like this becomes too much. I find myself slipping into that lost, defenseless child inside Roy's closet...then Alvin's motel room...then the police officer's car. Years after I've put my last instance of abuse behind me—after I've gotten an education and come into my own, feeling like a worthwhile individual and an adult who knows who she is—even after all this, I'm back to living the same tormented, lonely, damaged story of my past.

The strength and self-esteem that I've built up over the last decade disappear. Every time CO Brown grabs me, my mind wants to go numb. I begin to black out. The little girl inside wants to escape again, but this time, I have to hang on to my mind and my emotions. I need to stay present for my daughter's sake. *No, no*, I tell myself. *I can't fall. I can't sink into his horror, his craziness. Adrienne needs me!*

Because he has the same problem staying hard that Roy used to have, CO Brown doesn't actually penetrate me. Forms of sexual abuse aren't about sex or gratification: they're about power and control. Domination of any kind hurts and manipulates the mind more than anything. Predators target the most vulnerable, and CO Brown knows that as desperately as I need to help Adrienne, I fit in that category.

I fight depression over the course of the months that the sexual abuse endures: *Everything bad has happened because of me.* Just like in the days of my childhood, I own this. Though I manage to continue to stand up for Adrienne, I don't feel that I deserve to stand up for myself. On a deep, visceral level, I believe that this mistreatment from the officer is my punishment for having failed to protect Adrienne in the first place.

Finding myself again inside a dark trap, I finally build the courage to pull aside an officer whom I trust and share that CO Brown has been threatening me, but this quickly backfires. On Christmas Eve in 1995, four months after Adrienne first came to me about her own rape, a team of officers enters my cell and tackles me to the ground. CO Brown steps in, clearly having ordered this, blocking me with his shin across my chest, placing one hand on my forehead and using his other hand to stick his pen inside my mouth. As I writhe and struggle to get my breath, one of my teeth breaks against CO Brown's pen. The inside of my mouth bleeds for several days, and CO Brown writes up a report that I assaulted staff.

As punishment, I'm sent back into the Box.

Alone, again, I go nearly out of my mind. After all the positive changes I've made here, I have slid back down to the bottom. Now I'm completely disempowered from helping Adrienne. I can't even communicate with her.

I agonize with worry. The nightmares are constant. In my loneliness, I seek out the voice of a woman living next to me, but this time there is no Judy Clark. I try to imagine the feeling of having that friend close by, but I'm suddenly haunted relentlessly by a memory from the month before I ran away to Philadelphia with Alvin.

It started when Mr. Harris invited a few of my classmates to come to his house for a pool party and go out for pizza one of the afternoons during my stay with him and his wife. With Karen, a friend from school whom Mr. Harris had invited, I laughed and played in the water while Mr. Harris barbecued. After we'd finished swimming, in the bathroom, Karen showed me how she used a hair dryer to style her hair. I stood in admiration as Karen used a brush to make her hair look smooth and shiny. I was so taken in to learn a style so different from what Daphne always insisted I should wear to make me look like a child.

Before she left that evening, Mr. Harris said that he'd bring her back in a few days and treat us to pizza, ice cream, and a movie. I looked at Karen with wide eyes, thinking how lucky we were that he chose us to spend time at his house that summer.

"Donna," Mr. Harris told me the next day, "I have something to tell you. It's not good." I remember fearing he was about to tell me that I couldn't babysit for him anymore, but he quickly assured me: "No—you didn't do anything wrong. This is about Karen."

I looked at him, puzzled.

"Last night, Karen committed suicide."

"What?" I whispered, searching his face in that way children do when our very basic human instincts suggest we understand what this means, even if we've never learned the language for it.

"Donna," Mr. Harris said. "Karen killed herself."

"But...why would she do that?" I played back the past twenty-four hours: I was just with her, we had plans to go to the movies. When I looked up again at Mr. Harris, his face was solemn. "Why do people commit suicide?" I asked him, quietly.

I watched as he tried to work out some explanation, though on some level I already knew that no one could fully make sense of this. "Sometimes people are depressed," he said, "and there's a lot of peer pressure. Or sometimes there can also be something going on at home that people don't know about."

It's here I remember thinking: *Maybe Karen was getting hurt at home, too.*

And my next thought followed—*Is killing yourself the answer?*

I began to wonder what my friend had been experiencing inside her private world; I wished we'd had more time together so that I could have shared more about my life to let her know she wasn't the only one suffering. We'd talked about my going away to boarding school—did she feel sad that I was about to leave? I became nauseated with regret, unsteady with all the questions and uncertainty; I even had a feeling of betrayal, some notion that maybe I perceived us to be closer as friends than Karen did. Did she know yesterday that it would be our last time ever seeing each other?

It was just days after the suicide that Mr. Harris pushed himself into the bathroom while I stood there covered in only a towel. My childhood was a constant search to find a light, something to make my surroundings less scary and unpredictable—and someone always interrupting my search, taking my hand in a promise to lead me faster into the light, but then dragging me into a deeper darkness.

My story of losing Karen unearths another memory that I'd buried, a time I'd witnessed someone else take their own life. I was about ten years old, home in Boynton on a weekend morning, while Daphne ran errands and Roy worked in his bedroom. Alone, I stood on our balcony, as the echoes of screaming and laughter from children in the playground below bounced between the brick buildings in our neighborhood. Suddenly, a person dropped in front of me and hit the ground. In a fraction of a second, it occurred to me that I knew him.

He lives four floors above us.

He landed on the sidewalk below in a lump, a moment so vivid that I swear I can still hear even the fabric of his clothing hitting the ground. There was blood everywhere, a small scatter of neighbors below calling out in shock. *He just killed himself,* I remember thinking.

He found a way out.

Disturbed, in shock, I stepped silently inside the apartment. After a moment, the sound of crying sirens blared. I thought of Daphne, who only stopped to speak to the neighbor women when there was a tragedy for her to weigh in on with her psychological expertise, when there was someone to judge for their public flaws. I thought of Roy down the hall, needing someone to reassure me . . . to hug me and tell me that I'm safe.

Instead, he took me into the dark. By this point, I was never safe at home with Roy. Inside the closet at his hands, I continued to stare at the light to try to escape. By now, the abuse had been going on for more than a year, and feeling so disgusted with it—with myself, my own body—I'd begun to try to resist. He responded with increased aggression, turning household objects into weapons to threaten me. He'd begun to hold me down on the bed and wrap his hand around my throat. Often during the rapes, I thought of our neighbor, who jumped to his death. Daphne and the neighbor women would gossip about it for weeks.

But I knew that our neighbor had found his own solution.

Awake in solitary, I suffer from anxiety, wondering what's happening to my daughter and playing back the story of my life, reliving each chapter of abuse. The years of progress I've made in my healing have been snatched away—again, by a man who had power over me.

Desperate for some outlet for my anguish, I begin to journal every single day. We're not allowed contact with any victim's family, but instead, I write letters to God asking Him to facilitate forgiveness from Mr. V's loved ones toward me. Here, I pour out all the things I wish I could tell them:

Dear Mother God,

I am writing to you in hopes that you will help me deal with and overcome this heavy despair that I am feeling right now! I am asking you to please forgive me for the part I played in Mr. Vigliarolo's death. I am asking you for mercy, Mother God, and for strength. I am asking you to send blessings to Mr. V's family and most of all to send them—to me—and everyone: PEACE!!!

I also pray that Mr. Vigliarolo forgive me, and everyone, involved in his death. And I pray that he is at peace also!

For eight months, I'm left alone with my emotions and my mind, which are far more confining than any four walls that could ever surround me. My only consolation is that in solitary, I'm safe from CO Brown's sadistic hands.

When I'm released from the Box in 1996, Adrienne's case still has not been decided. When she and I finally have an opportunity to speak, again I express my support if she wants to pursue charges. My spirit is crushed when she tells me that because I'm the only one who believes her, she feels too alone and too afraid to relive the trauma of what happened to pursue the case any further. Meanwhile, as I try to determine how I can best help my daughter, CO Brown continues to harass and accost me—he's relentless. Now there's also another inmate from whom I'll need to protect myself because she seems to have developed a love-hate obsession with me. Shortly after I'm out of the Box, I arrive back at my room just in time to find a plastic zipper-lock bag that's been slid under my bed.

Carefully, I open it up and gently shake the powder of black specks before I lower my nose to take a small sniff: it's black pepper, but it might as well be cocaine. Pepper is contraband and in demand because women will do anything to make prison food more edible. There's talk among the officers who say that if I get in any more trouble, I might be the first woman ever to be sent to Southport Prison, where every prisoner is kept in solitary confinement. After the eight months I've just lived through, there's no chance I'd make it out with my sanity intact.

Immediately, I take the stash straight to the prison authorities. A few have in fact been aware of this inmate's apparent agenda, and Superintendent Lord stands up for me. Even in spite of my shortcomings, she knows who I am inside and that for the past couple of years, I've been doing my best in the face of a lot of family difficulty. Superintendent Lord and I no longer see each other by our prison labels. We're two women trying to make sense of this place—our secluded little piece of the world where life is hard by definition.

I'm further encouraged to continue to tell my truth when a very unexpected figure becomes a regular at the prison. In 1996, there's murmur throughout the prison that Tony-Award-winning playwright Eve Ensler is going to visit the prison with the actress Glenn Close. Rumor is that the two of them are working to develop a screenplay about the life of Sr. Elaine. Many of us have heard of Eve, who wrote an enormously impactful Off-Broadway one-woman show, *The Vagina Monologues*—a compilation of women's true stories about rape, sex, incest, genital mutilation, and the Everywoman's journey to learning to love womanhood and her body—even *that* part of our bodies, no matter what we've experienced that has led us to feel ashamed, hurt, or humiliated.

There's always a lot of buzz when a celebrity visits the prison as an activist or to do research for some type of project or production, and this place is pulsing with energy as we wait for an update about the movie project from Sr. Elaine. What we learn, however, is that the plans for the movie have fallen to the wayside. We're all disheartened, until we learn why: Eve Ensler is struck by the women here, and she's expressed her interest in focusing on a different type of project.

By 1997, she begins to volunteer with us, hosting what we come to refer to as the Bedford Hills Writing Group, which is composed of about ten of us who are chosen by Superintendent Lord, Sharon Smolick, and Eve herself. Pamela Smart, Kathy Boudin, and Judy Clark are among my peers in the group. We meet weekly, gathering together around a large oval table and using pens and paper to write essays, poems, and stories about our lives.

It's clear that Eve is a specialist at getting women to dig deep and pull our most terrifying feelings and memories to the surface. For those of us in the Family Violence Program, Eve goes an extra layer deep and really gets us to look at the ugliness of what we've experienced. As difficult as it is, it's also one of the most therapeutic, healing, cathartic experiences of my life—like pulling the bullet out of a gunshot wound so that the tissue can begin to regenerate and heal.

One early assignment is for us to share what stories the scars on our bodies say about our lives. Another assignment, titled "If These Walls Could Talk," encourages us to reflect and open up on what we would learn about ourselves if the walls of the prison and the walls we've put up inside ourselves were all to come down. I write about something that very few members of my family here know about my past: my unborn child, who was ripped from my body just months before I found myself in jail. When my hands should have held my infant, they were cuffed behind my back.

When I read the assignments in front of my class of peer witnesses, there's so much about this act that gives me strength: their eyes on me as I voice my truth, hearing my own voice read words that I've written out loud, and getting this past that's lived inside me up and out.

Then Eve challenges us to write on this whenever we're ready: "If you could talk to your victim or victims, what would you say?"

I think about my letter to Mr. Vigliarolo, how I wanted to help him but didn't know how, and how I didn't want him to die. But when the ballpoint of my pen touches down on the page, what comes out is the very simplest, most honest truth about the way I've felt for the past twelve years:

Dear Mr. V,

I am sorry. I'm so very sorry. I will never be able to tell you how sorry I am.

I wanted to help you. I didn't know how, because I didn't know how to help myself.

Burning with emotion, as part of the assignment, I go on to pen a letter to Mr. V's nephew who's said to have been a very close family member. My message to him is the same: I am so sorry for how my actions and inactions hurt the person you loved. I will never be able to fix what I did, and I live with that knowing every minute of my life.

Writing these words and then reading them for others to hear is a tremendous emotional release. It's a unifying experience, a coming together of my inner and outer world, a wholeness that slipped away from me. This way of acknowledging my actions, directly to Mr. V in some sense, becomes the opposite of detaching: it's embracing. It teaches me how to feel the hurt of what happened to my daughter and me without blaming myself, without shutting down, without trying to find some escape. The writing exercises have a way of helping me process all that's happened, rather than continuing to be hard on myself for the fact that I'll never be able to forget it.

As a group, we invest ourselves deeply in Eve's assignments. Each of us is serious about understanding, coping, and reconciling with our roles in our crimes and the abuse in our lives. We want to be examples of what happens in women's and young people's lives when they feel they have no way out and no healthy choices. And we want to be vessels to a time in our society when women will no longer be forced into any type of act for which they'll later live with shame. After a year of these therapeutic writing workshops, I'm ready to put my words where my mouth is and use my voice in a way I've never had the courage to do before. In 1998 when CO Brown comes at me again—after three years of his abuse and the experience and growth I've had in the writing class, I cannot be silent any longer. If I want my daughter to continue to speak her truth out loud, then I have to do the same myself. "Fuck this!" I yell at CO Brown after one of his bully assaults. "NO MORE!"

I march to the lieutenant's office in the administration building to find that he's not in. "You can leave a message for him," says one of the workers in his office.

"No," I tell her, sitting on the floor in front of his office. "I'm not moving until he comes back." His staff looks around at each other but honor my insistence. The lieutenant has told me in the past that he regards me like a daughter. For this once, I need a father figure to step up and protect me.

When he returns, he and his staff surround me while in a very loud, clear—but calm—voice, I announce to his entire office: "The next time CO Brown tries to put his dick in my mouth, I'm going…to fucking…bite it…*off.*" This is officially the last day in my life that a man will ever, *ever* hurt me again.

After I state my complaint, other women in the prison begin to come forward with their own similar experiences with prison staff. As more and more open up about what's been happening in the darkest corners of the place, we realize that many of us have kept our shame secret even from our sisters. If there's anything we should know by now, it's that this has to change. Speaking out is the only action that truly has the power to bring sexual violence to an end.

11

CHANGING MINDS, CHANGING LIVES

On December 31, 1999, we all stay up to celebrate the turn of the century by banging pots against our cell doors and cheering through our tiny windows so that our breaths make fog in the night. As the clock strikes midnight to call in the year 2000, there's a resounding exclamation throughout the prison:

Happy New Year!

We've heard that the Y2K computer virus could cause a world-wide technological meltdown, and there's a half-joke around the prison that maybe our cell doors will open, and we'll all be set free.

I can still believe in magic, right?

While we all know that this is unlikely, I move into the new millennium feeling a new kind of freedom inside me. A powerful personal shift seems to have happened, thanks to Eve Ensler's writing group. Those exercises helped me reach one accomplishment that I haven't been able to access for myself: forgiveness. For the first time, I no longer hate that remaining piece of myself for some of the mistakes in my past. I've even stopped having nightmares.

Another source of emotional torture has slightly loosened its grip on me, as Adrienne is safe. She's also in the process of working out her direction for her life, as shortly before her eighteenth birthday, she asked me to sign her into the United States Army. It's difficult for a parent to think of his or her child putting her life on the line, but if this is what Adrienne needs to feel strong and protected and to continue to grow—if this is her chance to get away from Alvin, and especially if this is her chance to get an education—I support it.

Around this time, a spiritual shift seems to begin inside Bedford as well, with a few of my greatest influences in the prison beginning to leave us. After twenty-five years in prison, Betty Tyson has been New York State's longest-serving female inmate. She continues to hold a special distinction in my heart as my first prison mother... but now, we're nearing the time when we'll all have to let her go because a judge has determined that a report about the crime that Betty was accused of was wrongfully suppressed by the police. Time and again, Betty has proclaimed her innocence and has had a great deal of support from the public and even some members of the media. Now, she's the first woman in New York State to have served such a long time and ultimately been exonerated.

I experience both great happiness and a tender tinge of sadness when she is released. How has such a good woman lost so much valuable time here for a crime she didn't commit? But right now, that's not what's on my first prison mother's mind. "I can't wait to get home to my mother!" she says, squeezing me into a warm hug. "And to put on a nice pair of high heels!" (High heels had been outlawed in New York State prisons several years earlier.)

When we pull away from our embrace, everything about Betty's departure makes me wistful. Whenever a member of the family leaves, it's a little bittersweet. My heart is thrilled for them, but I'll miss them dearly.

In so many ways, Betty Tyson has shown me what's possible. The morning we watch her walk out of Bedford tall and sure, I'm beginning to believe that I might have the chance to put on my own high heels again one day.

In 2000, the next to go is Elaine Bartlett, who has inspired all of us with her courage and her strength as a mother. Elaine was charged with a first offense felony for selling cocaine and has become the poster child for protests against New York's 1973 Rockefeller Drug Laws, named after Nelson Rockefeller, who was governor at the time the laws were adopted. The laws were controversial with their dated, harsh statutes regarding the sale and possession of narcotic drugs. Elaine rallied a lot of public support and attention, and eventually celebrities like Charles Grodin, Susan Sarandon, and Russell Simmons involved themselves in the fight and led demonstrations to push for reform of the laws. Some of them have even come to Bedford to spend time with Elaine in the visiting room.

Elaine's story has brought many people together, but the relationship that she and I have is particularly isolating. The two of us had a rocky start in my early days, when she got into a fight with one of my friends and I tried to pull her off. An uncertain period began that to me was senseless, and Elaine held a grudge against me for many years. I understood that she was fighting for clemency and to return home to her children, and eventually, this became a common denominator that brought us together and reopened our hearts to each other and our shared reality. The whole time, I've *wanted* Elaine to go home. As she departs, I'm thankful we were able to revisit a friendship…a sisterhood. Not long after Elaine's departure, Kathy Boudin is released on parole, too.

As we lose members of our prison family, other women begin to enter. In the summer of 2000, Sante Kimes arrives at the prison and is assigned to my unit. She's been convicted of two murders, robbery, violating anti-slavery laws, forgery, and a number of other crimes with her son, who's twenty-five years old. I'm the unit representative, whose role it is to greet incoming women and orient them. Sante is old and frail but has a boldness about her that doesn't make her seem very remorseful for the crimes. "Oh, I'm innocent," she tells me. She tells me how beautiful I am—always a red flag for me—and asks for my help in writing legal documents. One of the correctional officers warns me to stay away from her. "She's very manipulative, and dangerous," the officer says. When Sante requests that I write letters from her to her son, I know to keep my distance even more. The court ruled that she and her son aren't allowed to have contact, and I have no intention of getting involved with that.

My focus is to stay positive and move forward to change lives—for other women, for myself, and for my daughter. When I meet one of the most sexually driven women during my time at Bedford, I'll feel called to stay this course. Teenager Amy Fisher, known in headlines as "the Long Island Lolita," who shot the wife of her thirty-five-year-old boyfriend in the face, has moved into a different unit than mine, and within a few months of her arrival many women in my unit begin to hear about the sex-crazy girl with the prima donna looks. When she's placed in my unit, one of my friends comes to me. "Hey," she whispers. "Amy told me she wants to have a threesome: me, you, and her."

I don't pay the proposition any mind. Having recently studied behavioral sciences and given some informed introspection to my own life, I gather that what might be at work under the flirtatious exterior of someone like this is a history of childhood molestation. I don't hold it against Amy—if any of us wants compassion for the wounds of our past, then we have to treat another with that same compassion—but I politely decline to participate in anything like what's been proposed. Soon, Amy and I grow to be friends who exchange secrets about makeup and talk about clothes. It becomes clear to me that she's struggling with a theme that so many of my Jail Sisters and I have had to work through: the bond between a mother and child. Amy worries about her mother and often hurts for what she's put her through. She misses her mom, and both the woman and the mother in me note the little girl filled with love and innocence, who's aching to resolve the wounds that come from having been brought up in an abusive household.

I persist out of my compassion for Amy and so many others, including my daughter and the child still living inside me. To this end, I've accepted an invitation to contribute material about my experience with Helen to the writing of a book, *Breaking the Walls of Silence: AIDS and Women in a New York State Maximum Security Prison,* for which Whoopi Goldberg writes the foreword. With several other women, I also take part in the production of a public broadcast announcement entitled *We Are Not Who You Think We Are* to educate the public about the signs, words, and body language that are indicators of abuse. Inspiring and supporting other women has emerged undoubtedly as my true calling and the reason I exist.

In 2001, I'm gratified to play a part in bringing college education back to prison when I'm a contributing writer and researcher for a collaborative study conducted by the Graduate Center at the City University of New York under the direction of Dr. Michelle Fine, a distinguished professor in social psychology, women's studies, and urban education. In partnership, our core group of change-makers at Bedford—including Kathy Boudin, Judy Clark, Pamela Smart, Iris Bowen, Migdalia Martinez, "Missy," Rosemarie A. Roberts, and Debora Upegui—write about the effect that college has on prisoners in terms of rehabilitation, remorse, taking ethical responsibility, and positive post-prison outcome.

This study allows the public and the legislature to understand that education plays a vital role in the rehabilitation of people incarcerated, especially when they have already served a significant amount of time in prison. Education changes minds as it gives these people skills that are marketable and sustainable, and also gives them a sense of their crime, the role they played in it, and the damage they've caused. Even if they committed a crime under threat, they can understand the events, relationships, and patterns that led to that. In the future, they can make a better choice. The study also shows that it's actually more cost-effective to release an aging individual with an education versus to keep them in for life.

When the study is published, it's called *Changing Minds: The Impact of College in a Maximum Security Prison*.

The statistics in the report proved education is a worthwhile cause: since the college program at Bedford began in the mid-nineties, one in every five of the 850 inmates has pursued college or postgraduate degrees. Of the inmates who attend college in prison, only 7.7 percent return to prison (an occurrence that's known as "recidivism"), compared with 29.9 percent of inmates who do not attend college. After graduation, one student says, "I was able to bloom in a very dark place."

After the report is finished, it's distributed to every governor in the United States and the departments of corrections in select states to gain support for college programs in prisons across the country. Many policy makers who read the report realize that they've taken away something that's proven to drastically improve their communities and our society.

The *Changing Minds* report accomplishes what we hoped, and more: a bachelor's program and an associate's program return in an initiative that Bedford Hills refers to as the Center for Redirection Through Education, which also has an arm outside run by Thea Jackson and her husband, Bailey Jackson. Together, the Jacksons work to get funding and universities to be part of the college consortium that's providing us with the program curricula and credits. In 2000, Marymount Manhattan College establishes a master's program that combines women's studies and English literature. I register for the program as soon as enrollment opens.

In our now four-year-running writing group, Eve Ensler sees how we're taking the initiative and using our personal stories to shape the world outside. This is when she organizes many of the poems and essays from our writing group assignments and compiles them into a script. Then, she does what we might not have dreamed: she brings together some celebrity friends to read our stories onstage at Lincoln Center in Manhattan. Actresses like Marisa Tomei, Glenn Close, Rosie Perez, Ossie Davis, and Hazelle Goodman perform in the show. The production, which Eve has aptly titled *Borrowed Light*, raises $163,000 for the Center for Redirection Through Education. This ensures that more incarcerated people will have access to a better education.

Shortly after, Eve brings in her group of actress friends to put on the same star-studded performance in the prison gym as the one that was held at Lincoln Center. This time, as a collective group, we all want to effect an understanding among the women at Bedford so that all of us as individuals know: I am not my crime. I am not that one isolated moment in time, where one bad event led to another. I am not my mistake. I am not an object. We want the women to know that as children, as teenagers, or at any point in their lives, no matter when or how badly they experienced abuse, they are not alone. There are others who have been there, and who understand.

The actresses also sit down to meet those of us in the writing group and discuss our stories. I notice that as we open up, nothing seems to faze any of these famous, wealthy women. A few of them open up, while others nod in a sense of knowing that hits me. I finally realize: on some level, even they can relate to the experiences of abuse that we've shared. Like that moment in my first Family Violence Program meeting, I'm waking up to the fact that physical, mental, sexual, and emotional abuses are universal to many, many women. Our skin color, our education level, our geography, or our economic status: abuse is all too often woven into the very definition and experience of being a woman.

Before we all go out onto the prison gymnasium's stage, the actresses and our writing group gather in a circle and pray. When I take my place in the audience and the lights come up, my heart pounds in my ears as I wait for Hazelle Goodman to breathe life into my words. When I hear her self-assured, youthful voice speak, I feel a thrill: *I wrote that! That's my story!* When she finishes, I look around at the women surrounding me. They're smiling, clapping; our eyes are filled with tears. We've all heard our own words being recited onstage, which somehow brings my journey to a new point of validation. Literally and figuratively, these actresses have given our stories voice.

Eve asks if we'd like to turn our journey in the writing group into a documentary. We agree with a unanimous yes, as long as there's an understanding and a collective mission to be authentic—to ourselves, our victims, the world, and young people who are in positions similar to the ones so many of us were once in. *What I Want My Words to Do to You* goes on to receive a Sundance Freedom of Expression Award and a NCCD Pass Award. It airs on PBS and is shown in high schools, colleges, junior high schools, and community centers across the world. The stories that brought us to prison and for so long have disconnected us from the world have now strengthened and gained enough power to bond us with women and young people across the globe.

In 2003, when sexy photos of Pam Smart in a bra and panties on a prison bed are published in the *National Enquirer*, Pam tells us women and prison officials that an officer was blackmailing her and raped her. When she files a complaint about it, she's immediately placed in the Box for two months. Like they did regarding her trial, the media rip her apart, as do some of the women at Bedford. But because I know what it's like to be threatened by an authority at the prison, I grow angry. Why should she get punished for that? It's piling abuse on top of abuse, and it's not right.

A short while after Pam returns to the general population in prison, she files a lawsuit against the officer. If her allegations are true—and I know from my own experiences that they very well could be—the prison system is failing miserably. I hope one day I can do something about it, and I keep this goal in mind as I continue to work and study hard.

My master's program combining women's studies and English literature continues to evolve my awareness of my role in society. Also, especially from my years in the writing group, it's clear how much insight we can gain about our own lives when we listen openly to the stories of others.

We have a few particular volunteer professors in the master's program who instill their confidence in us in a way that continues to strengthen our belief in ourselves. There are central figures, such as the renowned coffee entrepreneur Barbara Martinson, who encourage us to respond to the material we're reading in a very personal way in order to take these stories' lessons out into the world with us one day. Barbara is instrumental in teaching us stories about women and identity in literature. Aside from the material, she invests her own wisdom and experience in us and gives me hope that I too might one day be strong and successful out in the world.

One of my favorite courses is called "The Search for Identity in American Literature." I read novels like Toni Morrison's *The Bluest Eye* and Ralph Ellison's *Invisible Man*, which both address race and identity, and *Wide Sargasso Sea* by Jean Rhys about a woman's struggle for control of her life after she's sold into marriage. I consume stories about incest, displacement, and the power struggles between men and women. In every single tale, there's something I can relate to, including Plato's *Allegory of the Cave*, about a gathering of people who spent their lives chained to a blank wall inside a cave. If oppression has been a theme in society for 2,500 years, it makes me want to fight all the harder to make more rapid progress.

For my thesis, I research the 1950s writer James Baldwin, whose stories and novels explored subjects that were extremely taboo in his time. *Go Tell It on the Mountain* is the story of a fourteen-year-old boy in New York who's coming to terms with his homosexuality as the stepson of a minister. I know the neighborhoods of Harlem where the story's set, and it strikes me how fourteen can truly be the tipping point between childhood and knowing one's own mind and person. *Giovanni's Room* is a tale about oppression and Baldwin's having lived most of his life in the closet—a closet that would have been every bit as imprisoning as the one in which I spent so much of my childhood.

James Baldwin died in 1987, the year after I came to Bedford. I feel as though he might have understood me, and I'm moved by his ability to write his truth so bravely against the backdrop of mid-century racial conflicts. What speaks to me most of all is how he deals with the lesser spoken, very human struggles inside an individual's heart.

In 2003, at age thirty-nine, I earn my master's degree. As I near my fortieth birthday, I dare to marvel at the distance I've traveled, even inside these walls. I was never that unworthy child, nor the kind of person who could ever stand by and watch another human get hurt. I was once a little girl, and then a young woman, with great promise and potential. A girl longs endlessly for love, and her personal strength needs to be fostered every step along the way. Maybe prison shouldn't have been the place where I'd be protected enough to develop all this, but it was. In life, it's never too late to become who we really are.

With the capacities of my mind finally fully evolved, 2004 brings me to the next step in my personal evolution. Kathy Boudin has left prison shortly after the airing of *What I Want My Words to Do to You*, and the impact of her friendship as a fully evolved woman with a purpose to make the world better continues to inspire me. I hunger for more understanding about myself, about life, and I want to continue to tap into this stream of inner peace that comes with personal wholeness and a connection to my true self, as well as a loving connection to others. With more free time now that I'm no longer studying, I begin to spend more time in prayer, meditation, and writing about my spirituality.

Throughout my time as a hospice worker, I've worked as an informal assistant to the prison's chaplain when she's ministering to a terminally ill woman. But in 2004, Rev. Maria Lopez, the current chaplain, asks whether some of my sisters and I would be interested in playing a more hands-on role. Instantly, I'm intrigued. Rev. Lopez explains: Who better than us women to provide pastoral care in the hospice setting? In a way, we've already been doing that for years.

Noting receptivity in me and a few of my sisters, Rev. Lopez brings a clinical pastoral education program into Bedford. Judy Clark, Pam Smart, some others, and I go through the program, learning to provide pastoral care to our sisters in hospice. We read books by Carl Jung and other thinkers in psychology, philosophy, theology, and spiritual psychotherapy. We learn more about how best to hold a shared presence and listen to the woman who's very ill, as well as be present for her family. For me personally, Rev. Lopez brings me to another phase in recognizing the humanity in myself, which makes me better able to recognize it in others. She teaches me that every human being is a book. Our lives are made of different chapters, but when we come to the end, what have we learned? How would we like our lives to be read? And how do we read others, even after they're gone? Do we look back on them with judgment? Do we stick them with conditions? Or can we love them wholly, for their flaws and their mistakes? Can this show us how others might be capable of one day loving us just as unconditionally?

As I'm pursuing the pastoral care program in 2004, the prison's administrators grant me permission to move into the honor housing unit, where I'll have my own room in an atmosphere that's more relaxed and private. I'm still an inmate, a prisoner, but this is quite a step in my journey and my autonomy. It's also a chance for me to work with something I enjoy: dogs. In this honor housing unit, I participate in a unique program at Bedford Hills that trains dogs as guide dogs for the blind and as detectors of explosives to assist law enforcement officers.

Over the next couple of years, Rev. Lopez deepens my understanding of the power of just simply being with another person, of respecting and honoring them in their space, of allowing them to know that they have someone they can talk to in order to simply share their story. Seeing how I embrace this approach, Rev. Lopez informs me that a position has come open. She tells me that she's noticed I'm someone the women are eager to talk to. "I'd like to help cultivate that, if you wouldn't mind," she says. "Would you be interested in coming to work with me?"

After I spend a little time praying about it, my response is an easy yes. Now, again, I go deeper into learning spiritual counseling, in a way where it's not guiding an individual or telling them what to do as much as it is to support them in their faith, in whatever stage or experience they're in.

My ability to maintain this loving, neutral balance is thrown into action in 2006 when an unexpected catastrophe takes place in the hospice unit. I'm working with a woman who's coming to the end of her fight with Parkinson's when a co-worker attacks a unit officer in the room. My ill friend is caught in the middle of it, so by myself, I jump in to protect both the officer and the patient, getting pummeled in the process.

A few weeks after the incident, I receive a Letter of Commendable Behavior from the deputy superintendent of the prison's health department. This feels good, but the greater reward is proof that even in a heated split second of danger, I truly have transformed—not into a different person, but like my thesis subject James Baldwin, I was just acting as the "real me" whom I know I've been all along. Had I had more faith in my own goodness twenty years ago, I never would have let those people hurt Mr. V.

12

WOMEN'S SEARCH FOR MEANING

In 2010, as I'm nearing the twenty-five-year minimum of my sentence, the politicians in Albany simultaneously encourage and disappoint us. With Sr. Mary, some other women, and myself, we've continued to work on the good time bill. The reason we're pushing for this with so much dedication is that New York is one of the few states in the country in which a person with life at the back of their sentence gets no consideration for any kind of early release. So many of us at this prison are proof of the potential that's possible when a woman is protected from a sexually abusive situation and given a chance to better herself.

Every time Mother corresponds with Albany about the bill, she informs us that things look very promising. There are constituents who are strongly opposed to this going through, but the politicians are coming to Mother frequently for recommendations and using language directly from what we've written and proposed to the legislature.

When New York State passes the bill, they have indeed used a lot of our ideas and our language, but the end product is a merit consideration policy that's far more neutral than what we've been driving for. Because Governor Paterson's goal is to avoid appearing as if his administration is opening the gates of prisons to let people out, they've passed the bill through with a much more conservative consideration than we'd asked for. The most that they'll allow a person with a life sentence to receive is six months off their minimum sentence. Mother is sorely disappointed, as are many of us. "At least we got the door open a little," I tell my sisters. "We have something to work with, and now we can go forward."

We're about to find out, because by the time the bill goes through, I'm the first prisoner at Bedford who is eligible to apply. When I do, I'm granted a merit hearing, in part thanks to what the prison administrators refer to as my "exceptional institutional record and adjustment." The prison administrators refer to me as "the model prisoner" and hope to make me an example to other women, demonstrating how going above and beyond to rehabilitate and improve ourselves in prison could come with a reward. To all of us, the possibility of my getting out early could show that there's progress in our justice system that would acknowledge us not just as prisoners to be punished, but as citizens with productive lives to live. For me, an early release also could finally enable me to forge a strong, permanent bond with my daughter and be present for her. She's been discharged from the military, but recently I've found it as difficult as ever to try to keep in touch with her. When I dug around to try and find her, I discovered that Adrienne has moved to Chicago . . . and she's battling a deadly heroin addiction. A pressure builds, and my head feels as though it might explode with worry as I beg God to help me out of prison. I remember Love, how that drug made her so vulnerable to life's most ruthless predators. Adrienne has already been through enough without her mother to help her. *My daughter needs me present to save her life now more than ever.*

By the time I'm approved and granted that merit hearing in December 2009, it's just one month shy of my initial parole board hearing, which is scheduled for January 2010 for the possibility of my release in spring 2011. We quickly learn, however, that because this merit time consideration is new to the state commissioners and the administration at Bedford, the decision on my merit time turns out to get extremely confused.

When your sentence is twenty-five years to life, after the twenty-five years are complete, it's standard that a prisoner goes for a parole board hearing, where a small handful of parole board commissioners will judge him or her all over again. The theory is that at this stage, the judgment will be based on eleven criteria assessing how the prisoner did his or her time. These criteria include the individual's institutional adjustment; the things they accomplished; degrees, awards, or certificates they attained; activities they were involved in; their disciplinary report; and other considerations along these lines.

Sadly for me and for thousands of other incarcerated people,

New York State is particularly notorious for flaws to this approach. Instead of assessing an individual's conduct during prison time, what they continue to focus on is the nature of the crime. It's understandable that they would give the crime some consideration, but after a period of time—certainly after twenty-five years—shouldn't they just weigh whether and how much the individual worked to change?

In December 2009 I report to the initial board hearing in front of three parole board commissioners—always an odd number of them, in case a tiebreaker on the vote to release me is necessary. What happens next is a devastation to everyone at the prison, including Mother, who has begun to work gruelingly with the Correctional Association of New York, specifically Tamar Kraft-Stolar, director of the Women in Prison Project, and Jaya Vasandani, Tamar's co-director. Together, they develop strategies and gather materials that could assist the parole board in making a decision in my favor, while people from the community who have supported me write letters commenting about my personal progress during my time at Bedford. To go with all of this, my parole officer is supposed to have spent a year preparing a packet for me that's meant to contain all of the technical records about my crime and my time in prison.

At the parole board hearing—always held on a Tuesday—the commissioners ask me if there's anything I want to say. I have thought a great deal about this, and I prepare myself to get it all across: I understand the part I played in Mr. V's death, but I didn't want him to die. I tell them that while I've been here, if I could have told his family how sorry I am, I would have. I also share that

I've worked very hard over the past twenty-five years to develop my mind to make better decisions and straighten out my life. "I own it," I tell them. And I'm sorry for my mistakes. Not another twenty-five years inside this place, or any amount of time at all, could take away the mental torture I will experience every day for the things I was part of long ago.

Three days after this, I'm in the recreation area when a sergeant comes around while all the women gather and watch his delivery to me with anticipating eyes. I've been at Bedford longer than most of them have been, just like Betty Gal Tyson and Elaine Bartlett were in for years before I arrived. What happens to me next could mean hope for many of them...or not. We all have a stake in this decision.

The sergeant hands me the envelope and my fingers fumble to fight with it, an eternity in only a few seconds. When I open and unfold it, indeed, it's a letter from the board.

And it's blank.

It's as if the entire recreation room sinks—into disappointment, confusion, dismay. I, personally, cannot feel a thing. Women gather around me and voice their support in a range of emotions that run from subdued to fiery. In response, I simply put on a strong face. I don't want them to be crushed.

The paper was supposed to have stated a simple *Yes* or *No*; *Donna Hylton will be released six months before her minimum sentence*, or she will not. In a way, the blank paper is even more of a letdown than a *No* would have been. It feels as though we're forgotten; it's an indication that the state doesn't even know yet how to implement the new policy that could lessen a minimum sentence. No one at the prison knows what to do. I do the only thing I can. I pray.

The following month, in January 2010, I return to the parole board for what had already been scheduled to be my first board meeting to evaluate whether I'd be released after fulfilling my twenty-five-year minimum sentence. From my twenty-five-year-thick packet, they read the singular paragraph that summarizes the crime. If they have a set of eleven different points on which to judge my release, why are they stuck on one that happened twenty-five years ago? I didn't murder anyone, but they don't hear that.

After this January 2010 hearing, I get not one decision in the mail, but two. The first one is from the limited credit time hearing that initially came back to me blank. Not only do they *not* grant me the limited credit time allowance, they've also added two years to my sentence. It's devastating to all of us—women and staff.

The second letter is from the January hearing before the initial parole board. Again, *they* hit me with another two years.

Now, it's triple confusion. There was a chance for me to leave prison six months before my twenty-five years were up...but now I have to serve an additional four years?

No one is more hurt than Mother, who says: "Enough is enough." The prison administration and the facility parole officer put in a query with the parole board commissioners, and there's a sigh of relief among all of us when they inform us there was an error. Then the prison administration and the state office of parole contact Albany... and yet another board hearing is scheduled.

In February 2010, I report for the hearing only to learn that some of my paperwork, the sentencing minutes from my 1986 trial, is missing.

I'm frustrated, perplexed, deflated. I was there when a man's life was taken—that's my role and my responsibility. Now all I'm asking is for the chance to go out in the world and be part of the larger societal solution to all the hurt and difficulty in our world.

Almost a year passes before they finally get all the confusion straightened out. Mother brings in a young but very bright litigation attorney to represent me. Jeremy Benjamin works for the Manhattan law firm Paul, Weiss, which is one of the top law firms in the country. I begin to feel guilt, wondering who could be funding this, until Mother tells me that Jeremy has taken my case pro bono.

Together they work very closely with Tamar and Jaya. Mother and I have approached both prison administrators and influential people outside, such as Eve Ensler, to write letters of support for me. On my behalf, Eve graciously writes:

> Donna has been honest in dealing with her crime...I was moved by her seeking spirit, by the depth of her guilt and her profound willingness to walk in the fire of reckoning. Donna is a smart, deeply compassionate woman. She has a gorgeous spirit. She has worked hard to become a new person in prison.

Bob Dennison—the former chairman of the board of parole— begins to visit me and becomes one of my biggest advocates, finally helping me to recognize my past with a perspective I haven't seen before when he writes a letter to state: *This woman was young, and she did not kill anyone.*

It has taken almost three decades and a great deal of learning, understanding, and therapy to help me heal. Now, Bob encourages me and gets me to understand: You can be responsible without being responsible. You can step up for your part without shouldering the fall for everyone who was involved. This idea brings a depth of healing I've sought for twenty-six years.

Mother's own letter for me states:

I have witnessed Donna struggle with her difficult past, make tremendous gains in confronting and reconciling with her childhood abuse, take personal responsibility for her past actions, with deep remorse for the consequences of those actions, and commit herself to improving the lives of those around her.

Even Alvin's mother, Dorothy, has written a letter that validates my experiences.

I have known Donna since she was fourteen years old. She lived with her adopted parents in the same building where I lived with my family.

Donna was an extremely smart girl in school. However she complained a lot about her somewhat miserable existence at home. This activity led to her running away with my son to get away from the abuse. The relationship resulted in the birth of my granddaughter Adrienne.

It will be a blessing to see Donna and her daughter reunited once again, as Donna went away when her daughter was still a tot.

Superintendent Lord also writes a letter on my behalf, stating:

Ms. Hylton has worked hard at self-improvement...She has truly matured and grown in prison and should now be in the community using the skills she has acquired.

The progress continues to build, and in late winter of 2011, things in my life start to feel a little different. Maybe it's my work in the chaplaincy and my own expanding spirituality, as I've even begun to study to become an ordained minister. But now, for certain, I very subtly begin to sense that something new is happening.

Around this time, a friend invites me to a Bible group. In my faith, it's customary to accept someone's invitation to attend a gathering for the purpose of worship because we believe there is one God of all. By now, Rev. Lopez has left here as the chaplain, and a new gentleman has taken her place for the interim.

There's something unique about Pastor Morris and the way he includes history in his Bible lessons. Since I was nine years old, searching for the answers, I gravitated to the Old Testament, Psalms and Proverbs—and here, Pastor Morris is able to put the teachings of God within a context of what the people were experiencing in that time and in their culture. I've read the Bible for almost forty years, but now I'm able to understand the relevance of its teachings in a much deeper way. Pastor Morris's understanding and passion for the Bible are contagious. Back in the unit, many of us women gather during our free time to review Bible passages together and discuss them in depth.

In March 2011—twenty-six years to the month since the crime went under way—I enter Pastor Morris's praise-type gathering, with gospel music playing and women worshiping with deep focus and connection. When I enter, I quietly slip into a pew and take a deep breath. As I settle into prayer, I suddenly begin to feel that there's something different about this day.

I glance around, thinking, *Is that the smell of roses?* I try to identify who's wearing this pretty perfume, but as I keep searching for the source, the scent is unmistakable: these are fresh flowers. Music is playing, filling my head and my soul; however, I don't see a single stem anywhere. I return my attention to my prayer, absorbing the music . . . but the fragrance does not go away.

The song that's playing begins to swell with energy—there's music, more music, just flooding the place. I notice that my vision can sense a certain kind of movement, an energy that my eyes can actually see. It's like a shadow—not very clear, but a force of physical energy that seems to be swaying.

The music builds and builds, and the smell of roses fills my senses. One by one, Pastor Morris stands before each woman, pouring a few drops of oil into his palm and placing his hand on each of our foreheads. Now, I've seen what happens when he lays his hands on someone: Sometimes there are women who scream and fall down like they're in pain. Some start to speak in tongues, and this always makes me skeptical. I can't help but wonder if they're faking it, showing off for attention. It doesn't seem real to me.

But now, with my palms pressed together and my head bowed, Pastor Morris comes to me. Tears have begun to brim in my eyes as the music plays strong, and there's this feeling in me, so honest and open—

It's pure love.

I'm focused devoutly in prayer, but filled with awe and amazement about the love I'm feeling. Something is very different.

Pastor Morris pours oil inside his hand and places it on my forehead. Nothing happens; it just feels nice to feel the warmth of his hand and the gentleness of his touch. The music continues to play, and the smell of roses is now so strong it's impossible for me to accept that there's not a big bouquet sitting right beneath my nose. Around me, women screech and jolt under Pastor Morris's touch. *Dad*, I pray. *If you're real, and if you're present, then let me know.*

When Pastor Morris lifts his hand away from my forehead, I keep my eyes closed but can feel that he's still standing in front of me. Again, he places his hand gently on my forehead—and right then, a force rocks me backward.

It's powerful but gentle, and I have to open my eyes to stop myself from falling. *Wait a minute, what was that?* When I look up at him, Pastor Morris moves on to anoint the woman kneeling next to me.

Again I close my eyes and bow my head, tears still spilling down my face. *Dad,* I pray, *if that's you, please let me know. I don't want to be a hypocrite.* I become aware of a burning, tingling sensation from my lower right thigh, which runs all the way up my right side to my neck. My right side is filled with heat, but my body itself doesn't feel overheated.

Then, I hear something clear in my head:

I am here.

I gasp, and tears pour down my face. *Am I going crazy?* The smell of roses is to an extreme level. The heat builds and pulses from my thigh to my neck… and then I hear:

And I am pleased.

Now, I know: this is the Holy Spirit.

Pastor Morris takes his place at the altar and asks, "Did anyone know what just happened here?"

Somebody please tell me what happened here! "I smelled roses!" one woman calls out.

"Yeah," another adds. "I smelled roses, too."

"So did I!" I add. "It was really strong!"

Pastor Morris looks at me. "It was coming from you, Donna."

What?

"When you sense the strong scent of roses while you're deep in prayer, the Spirit is making its presence known to you."

This moment in March 2011, when I'm filled with the Holy Spirit, is a pivotal, life-altering experience. I know now for sure that the Holy Spirit is real, and there's no turning back from this knowing.

This day is the start of my visions and dreams. I know for sure that my life is changing—that I'm changing. Something is happening.

Throughout spring and summer of 2011, I continue with my Bible study courses and in the fall of 2011, I become ordained as a Christian minister. After a lifetime of searching my soul, I know now that Jesus has always been a constant for me. No matter what's happened in our lives, he loves and accepts everyone.

That October 29, my forty-seventh birthday, when I glance out the window of my cell, there's snow. It has never snowed on my birthday before, and it reminds me of the afternoon outside with Daphne, before the abuse by Roy ever started, when I experienced snow for the first time in a moment of pure, childlike wonder— a moment of innocence. "Snow precipitates from the sky, Donna Patricia…" Daphne had explained. I don't tell anyone, but to me, it's a very clear sign that another event is about to precipitate:

I'm going to leave prison.

From this point, I begin to wake very early in the mornings to give myself plenty of time before breakfast. I use this time to start my day in prayer, to meditate, to journal my dreams from the night before and the occurrences that are giving me clues: things are changing. There are little, subtle signs and clues almost every day. I go into periods when I fast from eating for a few days at a time to prove to God my faith that He will provide for me.

Jeremy, Jaya, and Tamar all continue to work tirelessly with Mother and me. Then, in December 2011, I appear once more before a parole board. This time, they ask me what my release plan would be if I'm allowed to leave Bedford. I tell them that Mother and Jeremy have assured me they'll arrange housing for me at Providence House, a transitional housing facility founded by

Sr. Elaine for women who have been newly released from prison. Altogether, I spend two hours with the board. "In all the years I've been doing this," says my facility parole officer, "no one has ever had such a long board interview."

When I receive the parole board's letter of decision, what I've known since that day nine months ago with the roses becomes true:

I'm a free woman.

On Sunday, January 15, 2012, as my parting gift to the women, I host the prison's Sunday services. To a standing-room-only chapel, I read from the Gospel of John, which says, "Greater love has no one than this, than he who lays down his life for his friends," and from Isaiah 61:1:

> The Spirit of the Lord God is upon Me, because the Lord has anointed Me to preach good tidings unto the meek. He has sent me to bind up the brokenhearted, to proclaim liberty to the captives, and the opening of the prison to them that are bound...

I share with them the most important understanding I've developed during my time here: that we can connect deeply with humanity if we look through the eyes of love and compassion. We have to treat each other with constant love, both here and out in the world. I also tell them that rulers, leaders, kings, government, and our justice system may too often observe what's known in the Bible as "the letter of the law," or the literal interpretation of what the law states. However, I tell them, it's our job to live by the spirit of the law and that God's greatest law is to love one another as He loves us.

I would be released the following day, except for the fact that it's Martin Luther King, Jr. Day—a significant detail in this ongoing fight for human rights. The holiday gives Pam, Judy, and the rest of my prison family the chance to shower me with mementos to help me remember them. Pam even gives me her favorite pair of leggings, hugging me as she says, "Wear these so that a piece of me will be in the free world with you. Maybe it will bring me good luck."

The next morning, on Tuesday, January 17, 2012, after I've been incarcerated twenty-six years, nine months, and two and a half weeks, I wake up and take a few minutes to say a prayer of thanks, and a prayer of protection for my sisters who will remain here. Then I put on a pretty black suit from Mother, and, thinking of Betty Gal Tyson, I slip my feet into a pair of high heels before I'm escorted by an officer toward the administration lobby. "It's so quiet around here," I tell the officer.

"There's a code blue," he says. "Partial lockdown." When I look at him with question in my face, he explains: "They were worried there would be a rush of women wanting to see you off."

At the front gate reception area, I accept a small package. In this moment, my past meets my present as I discover what it holds: a tiny pair of earrings, and a watch that my captain friend from Rikers gave me before I arrived at Bedford. In one way, time stopped for me when I came in here, and yet, so much in my life has changed. These two tiny belongings have been kept safely for me since I arrived at Bedford.

After I sign my discharge papers, an armed guard buzzes open a steel electric door as morning light from the bright winter day breaks its way inside. I step forward into the light of day, into a free world that I don't know anymore. Among feelings of exhilaration, sadness, bewilderment, hope, and uncertainty, I drop to my knees.

Thank you, God. Thank you.

When I look up, a figure I know well stands before me. In front of a small sedan with a smile on her face is Mother. She's come to pick up her girl and take me home.

13

CARRYING THE TORCH

As Jeremy Benjamin waits in his car behind her, I climb into Mother's Honda Civic—the smell of the inside of a car permeating my mind. I'm sure that for a long time, the most common experiences like this will fill my senses, dawning on me over and over how freedom is truly our natural state.

Ten minutes down the road from Bedford, Mother and Jeremy stop off at a diner, where I'm faced with the first of many decisions I'll get to make for myself: *What should I order?!* Mother and Jeremy assist me in ordering, though when we exit the diner, I'm so overwhelmed with thoughts and emotions that I realize I wouldn't be able to tell someone what I ate for my first meal out of prison.

After breakfast, I switch to ride with Jeremy, who takes me all the way into Brooklyn and sees me into Providence House. Here,

I'll be set up with a room and meals until I'm able to get on my feet. There will be so much to take care of in the weeks ahead: finding a place to live and getting set up there, finding a job, learning my way around the city again...even the thought of shopping for a wardrobe puzzles me. The first thing I do when I get time in the bathroom is take a long, hot shower.

That night, I don't sleep, but it's not because of excitement. The truth is, I feel scared, overwhelmed. Lonely. I need to talk with *someone*—with Mother, Jeremy, Jaya, Tamar, or Kathy Boudin, who's now working with HIV and AIDS patients at a hospital in the city. There's only one house phone, and we're not allowed on it past curfew. Without access to my friends, I feel like I'm still in prison. I still cannot believe any of it: *Am I really free?*

The next morning, Hazelle Goodman, who read my words as part of Eve Ensler's *Borrowed Light* production, arrives at Providence House at 7 a.m. and greets me with a hug. "I brought you some clothes," she tells me. "Go on and get ready. I'm taking you to report for parole."

The house manager at Providence House had me sign documentation to receive a complimentary subway card and told me that the train is just down the block, but I don't even know how to get there—and once I arrive, I don't know how to board the train. When Hazelle and I descend the stairs into the subway station, I don't understand why people around us are using plastic cards to enter the turnstile. When I left in 1985, we used tokens. "Here's how you use the MetroCard," Hazelle tells me, showing me how to swipe my ticket through the reader. When I ask her why people are walking down the street talking to themselves, she giggles. "They're on Bluetooth," she says. "People use cell phones now."

I try to take it all in with a little humor, but I feel like I've been thrust out here. It reminds me of a line from one of my favorite movies that we watched at Bedford, *The Shawshank Redemption*: "While I was away, the world went and got itself in a big damn hurry." I look around Manhattan, intimidated and overwhelmed, like I did when I was seven years old and arriving in this city for the first time. Now, I'm like Rip Van Winkle, having fallen asleep in one century and woken up in another. People rush and bump into each other, and look down toward the ground as they read and shop on the Internet and briskly send messages through their phones. No one sees each other. Nothing looks the same. Nothing *is* the same. All this newness has a way of overwhelming a person who's been locked up from the world for more than two and a half decades. On my second day out of Bedford, the outside world is so much that I have to stop and take a breather to prevent a panic attack. I understand now why it's normal for women reentering their communities to develop what's known as "jail sickness." When prison has been our longest stretch of a home, it becomes the only place of any consistency in our lives. We know the inside, but the outside is the unknown. A terrible headache sets in from all the stimulation and stress. When I step out just to see what it feels like to go out for a coffee, a woman on the street bumps into me with no apology while she's texting on her phone. Automatically, I ball up my fist in anger and disbelief. *What would she say,* I wonder, *if she knew I'd just come home after serving almost three decades in prison?* I think of Mother, of her commitment to us women—to me. I loosen my fist and again start my way down the street, knowing that this readjustment is going to require a lot of forgiveness for others, and for myself.

Two days after I arrive at Providence House, I begin to ease in and find my place when Mother asks me to speak at the John Jay College of Criminal Justice, where she's hosting a panel on women who have experienced abuse. I've only been out of prison for forty-eight hours, but in front of these students, I feel at home. Speaking about my life experience to make people aware of where abuse can lead feels like a very natural fit for me. "We share the same heart and mind for women's issues," Mother says after my talk. It's her way of affirming my courage to tell my story, our shared knowing that this sharing is one of the most powerful ways to help other women discern paths that are different and better than mine.

One of my first errands in the days I'm getting acquainted in the city is to send Adrienne a card. My message inside is simply:

I'm home.

A few days later, she calls me and says she knew when my inmate number wasn't listed on the envelope's return address, there had to be news.

That exact night, Adrienne boards a flight to New York. She comes to see me at Providence House and then spends over a week with Roy and Daphne, making trips into Manhattan to see me every day. "I just want to be around you," she tells me.

The following month, in February 2012, I accompany Mother to Albany to promote the passing of a particular bill that I worked on at Bedford alongside some of the other women and Jeremy, Jaya, and Tamar. The bill is known as the Domestic Violence Survivors Justice Act, and it addresses one of the major issues that has not yet been resolved: the fact that women who kill their abusers to protect themselves, sometimes even accidentally, are often given the same sentence as a murderer who kills out of pure malice, not as any kind of act of defense or personal safety.

Mother continues to act as my supporter, my advocate, my friend, my backbone. She drives me around the city to get me set up in helpful programs, and together, we try to figure out Google. She also helps to ease me into the beauty of freedom by taking me to the Bronx Botanical Garden to see our favorite flower, the orchid. We spend hours walking through the gardens and smelling the flowers. Mother reminds me that my spirituality and a sense of belonging to a community will be important as I continue to adjust to life outside. I agree and begin to seek out a place of worship, winding up in a church in Brooklyn not too far from Providence House. One of the parole commissioners who was on my board talks with the pastor of the church, who introduces me to a woman in their congregation, Wendy McClinton. Wendy is the president of the Black Veterans for Social Justice organization. "You deserve a second chance," Wendy tells me. I begin working in the housing department at her organization with men who have served time as convicted pedophiles. The challenge frightens me at first: I'll be face-to-face with men who have similar traits as Roy and those who hurt me during more vulnerable times in my life. When I start the job, I discover an effect on me that I could not have anticipated: this too has a way of healing me. For the first time, I'm able to see that most of these men who have hurt children learned abuse somewhere. In many cases, they experienced great suffering of their own. It doesn't excuse their behaviors, but it does help me develop a sense of forgiveness that I was never able to reach before.

This begins to validate for me that we all have that light, that little piece of God, inside us. We might do some messed-up things to each other because we're human beings, but that really doesn't mean we're bad people. We all have the capacity to be good. That's the way God makes us.

I remain living at Providence House until March, when I transfer to Mother's apartment where she lives alone in Harlem. She's constantly on the go with all of her commitments and her involvement in causes for women, but together we find quiet moments in the evening or early morning to pray together and discuss some of the challenges she's dealing with in her work. I begin to volunteer as an advocate at STEPS to End Family Violence, the program that she founded to help battered women. It's a role that builds my confidence, as it quickly becomes clear that this is the same work I was doing with women in Bedford.

After a month with Mother, a housing specialist from Providence House calls me. "My name is Rose. Do you remember me?" she asks me. "I was at Bedford for a while, and you were always so nice to me."

Of course I remember her, I tell her, and she informs me that an opportunity has just come across her desk: it's a vacant studio apartment in Brooklyn. "I know you've begun to work," she says. "Would you be interested in seeing the place?" I take the subway and find the apartment near the Brooklyn Botanic Gardens and just a few minutes' walk from Prospect Park, which is just beginning to bloom with signs of early spring. Inside, the place is clean, bright, and just the right size. When I apply to rent it, I learn I've been approved.

Mother donates a wooden table and chairs to me for my kitchen area, and the set matches my hardwood floor perfectly. People in our congregation and other people who know me contribute furniture and money to help me start out. I use some of the money to buy a futon bed, and I paint the walls a calming shade of blue. Over my bed, I hang paintings of seashells and ocean-blue seahorses, which call to mind the nature that I loved in my childhood. My apartment is cozy and comfortable and very close to the subway, making it convenient for me to get around the city.

Mother, along with friends like Jeremy, Jaya, and Tamar, all continue to support my reentry by teaching me basic skills, like how to write out a check and call the gas and electric companies to turn on my utilities. I realize how much Mother truly has played the role of a parent, protecting me, teaching me, and making sure I feel secure in my new life.

In the evenings and on free days, I take long walks in Prospect Park where I love to stroll beneath the trees and watch the swans in the lake. *I'm free.*

In October 2013, my job sends me to a conference in San Francisco—the first time I've been on an airplane since I landed in New York with Roy more than forty years ago, when I thought he was taking me to Disneyland. I explore San Francisco as a free woman, loving the architecture, the Golden Gate Bridge, the restaurants, and the way this city embraces all different kinds of people.

Sadly, this high period in my life will only be momentary. When I land back home in New York a few days later on October 18, I'm out walking when I get a call from Mother on my cell phone. "I have some bad news for you," she says.

Oh, no. Instantly my mind goes to something related to the women at prison . . . but what she tells me is actually worse.

"I had a few lumps in my neck that I went to have checked out," she says. "And the doctor tells me I have a rare form of melanoma."

Within a couple of weeks, she's admitted to Bellevue Hospital. I'm with her around the clock, spending the night with her and leaving from the hospital to go directly to work. A priest walks into her hospital room one evening, and Mother introduces me as her daughter. With a playfully perplexed look on his face, the priest replies, "Nuns don't have daughters!"

Mother raises her eyebrows. "This one does," she says.

In the second half of November, she's moved into the hospice unit. Along with her sisters in her community, she signs papers to give me the power to make decisions about her life if and when she grows too ill to make them for herself. She's already completed paperwork to donate her body to scientific research.

Mother's neck is now swollen with the lump, and the night before Thanksgiving, I can see that she's in incredible pain. A group of her sisters say a prayer before they hug her and wish her goodbye. Further into the night, her breathing changes. There's a rattle coming from her chest. She groans, and there's a deep gurgling that sounds from inside her as she struggles more and more for breath. "Is there water in her lungs?" I ask the nurse.

She nods. "She's in a lot of pain. It won't be much longer now."

I know she's right. I don't want her to go...but I don't want her to be in pain. Mother weakly motions for me to come closer. "Promise me," she says, "that you'll get the women out."

I remain there, silent for a moment. I don't want to lie—I can't do that to her. We both know the system we're all up against. "Mother," I tell her, "I promise you I will do my best to get the women out." She relaxes ever so slightly into her pillow.

I lean down to kiss her mouth, and I whisper to her: "It's OK, Mom. You can go."

I turn on classical music, her favorite (and still mine). I take a seat at her side and watch her face in angst, her labored breathing, thinking of all the things I'll miss about her. Her smile. Her unshaking love. Her candy. Her love of all things Irish, especially bagpipes. Her fondness of food and drink, and gatherings of family and close friends. Her favorite holiday: Thanksgiving.

On November 27, 2013 at 2:17 a.m.—on the eve of Thanksgiving—Mother passes.

Of all the sadnesses I've experienced, of all the people I've lost, losing this woman hurts me the most. I spent fourteen years looking forward to the day we'd be mother and daughter on the outside. Now, the only parent who has ever loved, wanted, and chosen me as a daughter is gone.

Three different memorial services are scheduled, including one at the Silberman School of Social Work at Hunter College, where she taught. Her official church funeral is held at St. Francis Xavier in downtown Manhattan, where the nuns have me listed in the program as Mother's daughter who will lead the congregation in one of her favorite prayers.

I notice there are eyes on me, and I'm not used to standing before crowds without Mother there. Fortunately, the priest breaks the ice when he tells the story from the hospital of the time Mother introduced me to him as her daughter: " 'Nuns don't have daughters,' I told her!" says the priest. "And Sr. Mary replied, 'This one does.' "

The story makes the congregation break out in warm laughter, including me. I approach the altar and take the podium, suddenly fighting back tears…but as I adjust the microphone, I'm overcome with calmness. *I know she's with me.*

Our congregation listens to a few of Mother's favorite readings, such as the Charter for Compassion, part of which states:

Compassion impels us to work tirelessly to alleviate all the suffering of our fellow creatures, to dethrone ourselves from the center of our world and put another there, and to honor the inviolable sanctity of every single human being, treating everybody, without exception, with absolute justice, equity and respect... We urgently need to make compassion a clear, luminous and dynamic force in our polarized world... Born of our deep interdependence, compassion is essential to human relationships and to a fulfilled humanity. It is the path to enlightenment, and indispensable to the creation of a just economy and a peaceful global community.

We also listen to a reading from the Gospel of John, chapter 15—the same reading I read to the women at my final worship service at Bedford: "Greater love hath no man than this, that a man lay down his life for his friends."

Mother devoted her life and her career to justice and the freedom, safety, and well-being of women. I know that there is no greater love.

That's why today, I spend my days working full-time as a community health advocate, assisting others who are transitioning out from prisons and jails. I also continue to spend my days, nights, and weekends as a criminal justice and prison reform advocate for people who are locked up, as well as those who are reentering society. I've started an initiative called From Life to Life—from *doing* life to *living* life. Through this organization, with help from others, I've been able to assist six women to date in getting released from Bedford Hills. Out of those six, four were terminally ill, and when they passed, I went to identify their bodies and helped raise money to bury them. For the others—one of whom is young Love—I met them as soon as they were out and provided them with clothes and a subway card or taxi fare. I fed them, gave them furniture for their apartments—all those details that are necessary when a woman is just starting out again. Combining my pastoral care experience with the more advocacy-oriented aspect of my background, I do for others what so many others have done for me.

I also remain an advocate and a voice for women's issues and rights. I may have left prison physically, but mentally and emotionally I'm still with my sisters on the inside, trying to help them. "Get the women out," Mother told me. Out here, that's what I'm working every day to do. I've become a voice for a campaign called Candles for Clemency, where each year, we hold a candlelight vigil outside of Governor Cuomo's residence, which happens to be just a couple miles away from Bedford Hills. Our group is often composed of many famous politicians and celebrities, and our goal is to push the governor to grant clemency to men and women who have been in prison for long periods of time but who have served their time with good behavior.

In 2015, I take the stage and open the event with a speech. But when I hear one of the governor's staff and another politician speak about the system, it seems as though they want the crowd to believe that they're already doing everything they can to grant clemency to some prisoners. *No,* I think. *There are so many women who need our help.* I think of the ones I knew who died in the Long-Term Care Unit after praying for release so that they could die with their families present. I think of a woman I went to visit at Bedford shortly after I was released. She had stage 4 cancer and had been the victim of spousal abuse, accidentally killing her husband while she tried to defend herself one night. She'd already spent twenty years in prison, and with the collective efforts of Mother Mary, a few others, and me, we got her placed in a nursing home where she was able to see her children and have a decent meal before she died. "I'll be happy if I die free," she told us, and she did—all while her family was given a few last precious moments with their loved one.

I go on listening to the speakers at the Candles for Clemency event, but all of a sudden, my head feels like it wants to explode— then it's as though the blast takes place on the inside of my skull. I think this could be one of my migraines, so I shut my eyes and try to brace myself, while the words coming from the stage continue to pound and ring inside my head.

As the next speaker steps to the microphone, I leave the front of the audience and walk to the back, holding my head in my hands until I go into the arms of the actress Kathleen Chalfant, who sees the way I'm cradling my face. "It's OK, Donna," she says, embracing me and speaking close to my ear. "It's OK." She thinks I'm crying from the intensity of the speech.

Inside her hug, I suddenly feel my body burning up. "I need air." Now alarmed, Kathleen helps me out of my suit jacket and lowers me to the ground. In a distant fog, I hear a quiet commotion surrounding me and a woman who says she's a nurse. An on-site EMT worker stands over me, and last thing I remember really clearly hearing is the word "oxygen."

Yes, I think. *Oxygen.*

Hours later, after some testing, a doctor informs me that I've had a stroke. I remain in the hospital for a week but am unable to walk or talk when they release me.

Nicole Scott, the correctional officer who treated me kindly from my earliest days at Bedford, comes to stay with me. For eight days, she cooks, feeds me, gives me my medication, helps me practice my physical therapy exercises, and gets me to the doctor for checkups. Two days after I come home from the hospital, Rev. Maria Lopez calls me. "I'm coming to wash your feet," she says. When she arrives, I'm fighting to do laundry and keep the apartment neat. Rev. Lopez urges me to sit down, and she kneels on the floor next to my feet. "We are here to care for each other," she says. "There is no greater love than that."

An even higher figure from my Bedford days also comes to care for me: Superintendent Elaine Lord. She's now retired and has recently won a battle with cancer, and apart from that, it's almost unheard of that a superintendent of a prison would do something like this for a former inmate—but that's the kind of person she is.

At this moment, neither Superintendent Lord nor I might have dreamed that in 2016, the former prison superintendent and I would appear for a television interview where we discuss some of the circumstances and realities for women in prison and their families, along with how reentry can be better for all of them, and for general society. "We're spending four times as much money to keep these women in prison than we'd spend if we gave them the best of services on the outside," Superintendent Lord says. "We could send a young person to Harvard for what we're spending to incarcerate [these women]."

We can't change the system alone, but we can encourage women to speak about the violence in their lives. The crime is often a symptom of a deeper problem—the violence in their lives—and Superintendent Lord and I repeat this to anyone who will listen. I didn't wake up one day and say, "I'm going to commit a crime today." That nineteen-year-old was so removed from the world, secluded in a dark, lonely, empty place with nowhere to turn and no one to talk to. Getting women to speak out about the violence in our lives could go a long way in reducing the number of crimes women commit and the number of women in prison—a figure that is increasing much faster than it is for men. Statistics also show that the ages of women going to prison are much younger than they were in my early days at Bedford. We live in an era when the future for girls should be getting brighter. Instead, it's growing darker.

In 2015, I took part in a public discussion with Piper Kerman, who wrote the memoir *Orange is the New Black*, on which the television series was based. After I shared with the audience the details of my own sexual assault, a woman in the crowd bravely stood and spoke for the first time about her own rape. I applaud her and honor her, because she's taken the first step to get help before the violence has a chance to escalate and take an even more tragic turn with someone ending up dead—either the victim, or the rapist.

Mass incarceration affects everyone, not just the person sentenced to prison. It breaks up families and impacts children who grow up so traumatized that they go on to repeat the cycle. Since I was released from prison, there have been bumpy moments as I try to reconnect and reconcile with my own daughter, who after my release moved from Chicago back to New York and earned an A+ certification in computers. She's shared some thoughts about her past, and our past. "The last picture in my mind that I have before your arrest was when we were on the train. You had on this blue, puffy coat—I think it was the wintertime. I don't remember where we were going, but I just remember staring at you. That's one of the few moments I remember having you, when you were free." It's a memory that I've kept with me, too.

Adrienne brought comfort to my heart when she revealed that even after I was incarcerated, she never doubted my love for her. She took a moment to fight back tears when she said, "There wasn't a day that went by that I didn't miss you—it was the hardest thing in the world. I used to almost hate to go to Bedford, because I could never take you home with me. I used to look forward to those visits, and dread them at the same time."

We discussed the time we had to appear in court, when she was that seven-year-old in jeans and a T-shirt, and she couldn't look at me. I always thought it was because she was angry at me or confused by her feelings, but for the first time, she recently shared: "The reason why I couldn't look at you was because of my father. When we went to the courthouse, he had me lie and tell the judge you were a bad mother. I couldn't look at you because I was ashamed to lie, and there was no way I could help you." It broke my heart to know that even as a little girl, she carried the weight of her father's lies and the burden of wanting to help me. Today, Adrienne says, "We're learning each other. That's what I want."

It shouldn't take thirty-six years or even a single day for a mother and child to have to relearn each other, but for too many families, this is life. When we work together to heal this part of our justice system, there's a good chance we will actually see crime rates go down.

Meanwhile, my prison family who are still inside live vicariously through me. I send them care packages and talk to them on the phone, chatting with Pam Smart almost every day. We have girl talk, where I tell Pam all about my life and she keeps me updated on what's going on in prison. Pam loves to hear every detail about the trips I take, what I eat there, whether I'm wearing her leggings. I do—in fact, I wore them on a recent trip to Los Angeles as I toured Beverly Hills. When I told her, Pam laughed joyfully. "You give me hope," she said.

In June 2017, just three weeks before I was scheduled to deliver this book to my publisher, I was on my way from Brooklyn into Manhattan when I bumped into an old acquaintance from Bedford. I'd taken care of her when I worked in the mental health unit, and she'd spent a little time working beside me on the utility crew that I created, and also in the mess hall, doing dishes and serving meals.

On a sidewalk bench in downtown Brooklyn, this woman sat alone and in disarray. I spotted her feet—bare, swollen—and when I looked at her face, I recognized her, but I kept walking.

Then something made me go back. How could I not acknowledge her when I know how it feels to be invisible? "Hello," I said.

She saw me . . . but in another way, she didn't see me at all.

"It's Donna," I told her. "It's me, Donna."

She heard me . . . but in another way, she didn't hear me at all.

I realized how, as visible as she was sitting on this bench, she was invisible to the world. As I stood next to her, everyone else continued to walk by her in disdain and disgust. I started a conversation with her, mentioning a few names of the women I knew she'd remember from Bedford. And then I told her my name again. She snapped out of her psychosis and in this moment of clarity, she recognized me. "Donna?" she said. "Donna Hylton?"

"Yes."

"You're free? I never thought you'd get out!"

For twenty-seven years, I considered telling her, that was my fear.

After we talked for a little while longer, she asked me for three dollars. I gave her a five. "Go get a pair of flip-flops for your feet, OK?"

When she slipped back into her psychosis, I wasn't sure if she heard me.

When I walked away, the run-in left me dazed . . . disturbed . . . and then, heartbroken. Here was a woman who was more oppressed by life outside—the baking summer sun, the concrete city heat, the neglect of society—than she'd ever been inside. At Bedford, she spent her days working on mess hall detail, doing our dishes and serving us meals. It hit me how she fed all of us women, but out here, no one was feeding her.

Her state of being tells me a lot about how our society treats people who need help. In prison, she was cared for. She was clean, clothed, fed, and given her medications. Free, she is homeless, off her medications, and dirty. Unloved, unwanted, and left behind. Is anyone looking for her? She is more than a number. Our society has grown callously indifferent to human life. Rikers Island itself has become the largest mental health hospital in the world. Jails, prisons, and detention centers are not the appropriate response to mental illness in our society. My friend's life on the street is proof: it doesn't work.

For Mother Mary, I will keep fighting for the humanity and the rights of the women both inside and outside. When I look back now, I see there was a reason she—my true mother—was so adamant to get me out of prison and involve me in her work: I think the day she picked me up from prison in 2012, she already knew that she was sick. *This is my daughter,* she'd told the priest inside the hospital. She never bore a daughter, and I never had a real mother. Perhaps it is our love, and not our blood, that makes us family. *Promise me you will get the women out,* she said.

I promised.

When she let go, I could feel her relief. She trusted me, and believed in me, and she's the reason I tell my story today...only it's not just my story. It's the story of far too many women. I aim to change that.

Some mothers leave their daughters jewelry or money, family recipes or traditions. My mother left me something very precious: She left me a better woman. She left me her legacy, a mission to carry onward.

We must keep working to get the women out—out of prison, and out of the cycle of violence in their lives and in our society. No matter what the past holds, we have to be part of the future solution.

We must also work to understand how the cycles of abuse and victimization are often two sides of the same coin. Even though I have been released from prison, knowing that Mr. V died as a victim in a senseless crime compels me to speak out against abuse and violence. We must understand the root causes. This understanding, compounded with compassion, will be the way to stop victimizing and abusing each other. Mr. V and every victim of these cycles are the reason for my advocacy; the reason I speak those uncomfortable truths. We can no longer remain comfortable— change will truly begin when we become uncomfortable.

And to that end, there is much more work to be done.

Hindsight has many benefits, freedom the most beneficial of all. I see now that some of the choices I made were part of a larger narrative—forming in the carefree laugh of a child, running barefoot through her island country, alone. Racing through fields toward the white sand beach, where she would drag her holey bucket through the blue-green waters hoping to catch crawfish.

It is with difficulty that I try to recall some things past and, when I do, I wish I had the unerring instincts of a child to have been able to discern those situations and people that would be the catalyst for the chaos about to come. The chaos whose origins had already established its root in an abused two-year-old body.

Somewhere in my memories lay the promise of redemption,

the possibility of forgiveness. Sometimes it is hard to articulate the interior struggles I have encountered—not because I can find no words, but because I get so flooded with memories, completely submerged in a history I would rather reshape.

Many of my childhood memories compose an impregnable wall I find difficult to thin out. At times, I am allowed fleeting glimpses of the little girl I remember. As much as she was filled with pain and hurt, tears and sadness, she was filled with hopes and dreams. With laughter...and with joy.

ACKNOWLEDGMENTS

First and foremost, I give thanks to GOD the "light" that is within us all. I would like to thank the "village" that embraced me throughout different times in my life, those who showed me what "unconditional" love truly looks and feels like.

Sr. Mary Nerney, you are the mother of my heart. Eve Ensler, you nurtured me as I found my voice. The sisters of my heart, Deborah "Denise" Banks and Nancy "Black Panther" Sicardo and Dalida Pullins-Clifton, your love and support warmed me on the coldest nights, your visits and packages nourished not only my stomach but my spirit. The women and girls of Rikers Island and Bedford Hills Correctional Facility, you opened my eyes to the sad reality of gender-based abuse and violence. Much gratitude and thanks to Mary "Tiffany" Johnson for saving my life as I was having a stroke, and later the teamwork of doctors including Dr. Rafael Ortiz, chief neuro-endovascular surgeon, and Dr. Suzanne Steinbaum, director of women's health at Lenox Hill Hospital.

Special thanks to (former) Superintendent Elaine Lord, Jaya

Vasandani, Tamar Kraft-Stolar, Jeremy Benjamin, Robert "Bob" Dennison, and the law firm of Paul, Weiss.

Very special thanks to: Dan Pearson, who believed in me and my story and encouraged me to tell my truth, the entire team of Dan4 Entertainment, Daniel Pearson IV, Max Zampieri, Thomas C. Harris, Lawrence "Tumbler" Davis, Jerry Davis, and Jayd Leaky-Daniels. Former correctional officers Stephanie Smagler and Nicole Scott: both of you didn't see me as a criminal but a human being worthy of love and forgiveness. My daughter, Adrienne; my agent and friend, Frank Weimann; my publisher, Hachette Book Group; my editor, Michelle Howry; and thanks to Kristine Gasbarre for going on this journey.

There are so many who've formed my "village," although not mentioned (due to space), who will never be forgotten or silenced.